ACING BYU

The Savvy Student's Guide to Maximizing the Undergraduate Years

Ben Black & Nate Black

SF TEMPLETON

This is not an official publication of Brigham Young University. The views and opinions expressed herein are the authors' own and do not necessarily reflect the views and opinions of Brigham Young University.

PUBLISHER'S LEGAL DISCLAIMER

This book presents a wide range of opinions about a variety of topics related to obtaining a university education. These opinions reflect the research and ideas of the authors or those whose ideas the authors present but are not intended to substitute for the services of a trained academic counselor. The authors and the publisher disclaim any responsibility for any adverse effects resulting directly or indirectly from information contained in this book.

BF Templeton LLC
8020 Duncan Lane
Boise, ID 83714
www.acingbyu.com
info@bftempleton.com

Ordering Information:

Orders by U.S. trade bookstores and wholesalers. Quantity sales. Special discounts are available on quantity purchases by corporations, associations, and others. For details, contact the publisher at the address above.

Acknowledgements

No man is an island, quoth the poet. In like manner, neither are two men the beginnings of an archipelago. We couldn't have written this work without the aid and encouragement of a lot of friends and family. And so we give thanks.

Together, we thank our editor Brittany Olsen for her many helpful suggestions and reigning in Nate's tendency toward sarcasm and overly dry and obscure humor; she cannot bear the blame for what remains.

We thank all of those who took the time to respond to our BYU-Provo Undergraduate Experience Survey, including Deb Black, Ammon Boon, Jason Bray, Joe Brewer, Jordan Faux, Spencer Gardner, Joe Hardie, Josh Keanaaina, Merrill Madsen, Dan McClellan, Ciara McCurdy, Allyson McFadden, Robert McFadden, Robert Mills, Ashley Rasmussen, Joel Rasmussen, Linda Reese, Aaron Sheffield, Rachel Sheffield, Steve Stay, Briant Transtrum, James Winfield, and Brannen Winn. You ensured that this book would be about more than just our own personal experiences.

Special thanks are owed to Josh Keanaaina for reading through the entire manuscript and giving many useful suggestions for how to breathe greater life into it.

Also, we thank our mom, Naomi Black, for reading through the full manuscript and, in addition to giving many helpful comments, doing what moms do best: encouraging us and helping us to believe in ourselves.

We thank Emily Remington for the fantastic graphic design work on the book, it looks awesome!

A huge thank you goes out to Jim Kasen, Mark Larson and Travis Blackwelder for all their excellent input and advice. This book would have been sorely lacking without their help!

Ben thanks his wife Claire for pushing him to finally finish one of the many crazy projects he's started and for her help and support while he slogged through many tough semesters at BYU.

Nate thanks his wife Deb for reading through the full manuscript, making many useful suggestions for its improvement, doing yeoman's work on the index, and for the many delicious cups of herbal tea in the late evenings when he was working on this book.

In spite of all the help we've received, all errors and omissions are ours alone. We both had a physics professor at BYU who gave a dollar for every typographical or content error found in the syllabus, exam booklets, or other course materials the professor had written. We couldn't possibly afford to give a dollar for every error identified herein, but we'd still love to hear about them so that we can continue to improve this book for future readers.

Contents

Introduction

We commend you on your choice to pursue higher education at one of the finest universities in the world: Brigham Young University. BYU is home to a veritable smorgasbord of both academic and extracurricular programs that will enrich your undergraduate experience and help prepare you for your post-graduation ambitions.

Our hope is to introduce you to many of the fantastic programs, organizations, and resume-building activities available to you at BYU. In the chapters that follow, you will learn about scholarships and grants to help you pay for school, ways you can get involved outside of class to gain real-world work experience, and how stand out from the rest of the crowd when applying for jobs and professional programs.

We wrote this book with two audiences in mind: future and current Brigham Young University students. Chapter 1 will help future students as they tackle the admissions process, whether as new freshmen or as transfer students. Chapters 2 through 15 cover a variety of topics that will help current students discover ways to pay for school, pick a major (and minor), increase both the quantity and quality of their writing output, study abroad, and much, much more.

Before we go any further, however, we ought to say a few words about what this book is and what it isn't.

What This Isn't

First, know that this book isn't an exhaustive treatment of every program, office, or service that BYU has for its students. We couldn't possibly include everything in a single volume and keep the information basic and accessible. It also isn't meant to be the final, or only, word on anything we've included.

One of the more obvious limitations is that our experience at BYU was limited to two majors, among hundreds. To address this, we polled friends and family, asking them to describe the things that helped them be successful at BYU. In doing so, we quickly learned that there are as many definitions, it seems, of success at BYU as there are BYU students. At the same time, we felt that there are some things that can be generalized to most if not all BYU students.

We chose the following as our definition of success at BYU: get in, get a lot done,[1] and get out, with an emphasis on the importance of mentoring relationships as a way to increase the number of skills developed, experiences obtained, and scholarships and grants earned.

What This Is
Now, a word on what this book is. First and foremost, this book is a beginning. We wrote it to bring together in a single volume a bunch of ideas for how BYU students can tap into a plethora of resources to make the most of their undergraduate years. It started out as an effort to distill all the things we'd talked about during Ben's undergraduate experience. From there, it grew to include ideas other BYU alumni shared with us as well as our research into all that BYU offers its students. Believe us, it's a lot!

In writing this book, we discovered the difficulties of including our experiences, which are both specific and lim-

---

[1] By *get a lot done,* we mean those things that will be most helpful in acquiring the specific knowledge and skills you need to succeed in your chosen field, *not* just a random collection of college experiences.

ited, while attempting to write to a general audience of future and current BYU students. We hope that this book is a conversation starter that will bring together past, present, and future BYU students to flesh out what we have done here by forming their own mentoring relationships.

You may have noticed that this book is coauthored by two brothers. Both of us graduated from BYU about 10 years apart. By the time Ben got started as a new transfer student, Nate had finished both a bachelor's and master's degrees at BYU. Thus, it was very natural that a mentoring relationship would form between us to help Ben with his studies.

After Ben graduated, he came up with the idea for this book, thinking that perhaps we could share some of our experiences with a broader audience. Before we get into all that information, we would like to more fully explain our individual experiences as mentor and mentee.

Ben's Thoughts
When I decided that I wanted to continue my Japanese language education after my mission, I began exploring different schools that offered a Japanese major. It was quickly apparent that BYU's Japanese language program was staffed by some of the most accomplished and renowned Japanese language teachers anywhere. After returning home from my mission, I was lucky enough to be accepted to BYU as a visiting student and then as a full-time student in early 2011. Sure enough, the Japanese program was phenomenal, and I was able to continue my language education with some of the most brilliant professors and students I have ever met.

While at BYU I was fortunate enough to have an older brother who could help mentor me my entire time at BYU. Nate's mentorship was invaluable in helping me make the very most of my time as a Cougar. He helped me learn about and get involved in some fantastic activities like undergraduate research groups, student council, and the Honors Program.

These activities elevated my undergraduate years to a truly world-class experience full of scholarship, personal growth, and a deep sense of accomplishment.

Without a little prodding, I may have never taken a closer look at many of the programs and activities that have since become some of my very favorite parts of my time at BYU.

Nate was the type of mentor that all BYU students would benefit from having. Having spent nearly seven years at BYU getting his undergraduate and first master's degrees, Nate was finely suited to introduce me to many of the people and programs that would make a huge impact on me during my own undergraduate years. To give a few examples, Nate introduced me to my first on-campus mentor, a graduate student, who took me on as a research assistant during my freshman year. Early on, Nate also recommended that I give the Honors Program consideration, which proved to be fantastic advice as you will find out in more detail in chapter 4. Finally, Nate made himself available to me as a sounding board which was extremely beneficial while I was considering which programs and other extracurriculars to be a part of.

Unfortunately, not everyone has an older sibling or friend with two degrees from BYU who can become their mentor. I hope this book will, in at least some small way, help serve as your mentor and point you to a few of the many exciting things that BYU has to offer, just like Nate did for me.

Nate's Thoughts

Growing up, I took it for granted that I'd go to college, but I never had a specific school in mind. During my junior year of high school, I tagged along with our older brother on a campus tour he took at BYU, which he was considering as a possible graduate school. I was favorably impressed, and when BYU invited me to visit the campus for a weekend the next fall, I jumped at the chance. At some point, I learned that all BYU students are required to take a number of religion courses and that pretty much convinced me that BYU was the place to be. It did not disappoint!

Ben has been very generous in his assessment of my role as his mentor. I love him because I'm his older brother (not big brother, since he towers over me and has been able to destroy me in arm wrestling since he was 17 and I was 24), and I was interested in his success as a university student in general and as a BYU student in particular since I got my own bachelor's and first master's degree there. So why wouldn't I talk to him regularly to see how he was doing and offer help and ideas along the way?

What began as a simple phone call and "Hi, how's it going?" developed into an ongoing, dynamic conversation about anything and everything that could help Ben succeed.

We never set a regular time, but we probably didn't let two weeks go by without talking, and sometimes we'd talk multiple times a week. Thanks to modern technology, almost 100% of our conversations happened either on the phone or via video chat because we lived in different states.

But if you must know my mentoring secret weapon, it was Ben. He has one of the best work ethics of anyone I know and is able to set and pursue goals with a tenacity that I both admire and envy.

In addition, Ben is remarkably adept at listening to ideas and advice and mining out the nuggets of gold (or even just gold dust) scattered amongst the rocks and dirt and then applying them to his specific circumstances to maximal effect. For example, in one of our earliest conversations, I learned that Ben had volunteered to be a test subject for a study being done in my old department. The study was being conducted by a PhD student that I knew when I was working on my master's degree. I suggested that, if he was interested, Ben should ask the PhD student if he needed a research assistant. I knew that in many cases, if not most, the answer would be yes.

Ben took that suggestion and not only became a research assistant to that PhD student—earning himself co-authorship on a peer-reviewed journal article and an abstract in the process—but also continued adding new research experiences in five other disciplines (Japanese, microbiology, ecology, computational chemistry, and library and information studies), gaining experience as a researcher in the sciences and humanities, boosting his science GPA, and earning grant monies along the way.

Again and again throughout his undergraduate program, Ben adapted our conversations to his specific needs and wants. By so doing, Ben amassed a wealth of knowledge, leadership experience, skills, and even wealth in the form of scholarships, grants, and the money he earned by starting a small business. Ben is very well situated to pursue his post-graduation goals of military service, medical school, and whatever else he sets his mind to do.

You will get the most benefit from this book if you will exhibit similar character traits as Ben did while I mentored him through his undergraduate degree.

Our Desire
As BYU alumni, our greatest desire for you is that you find success however you may define it, both at BYU and beyond. That's why we've written this book. If we make a suggestion that doesn't apply to you or is less than helpful, we won't be offended if you don't take it. But we are confident that there is something in this book for everyone.

Enter to learn!

CHAPTER ONE

So You Want to Go to BYU?

If you are nervous about your chances of being accepted to BYU, or you were denied admittance before and want to know how you can improve your chances of being accepted in the future, this section will give you a few proven tips to help strengthen your application.

These tips can increase your chances of getting accepted to BYU regardless of whether you are applying as an incoming freshman or as a transfer student. Just remember: There are many ways to climb to the top of a mountain, so take heart in knowing that there is a way for you to get into BYU.

Below is a poem that Ben found extremely encouraging when he was struggling to learn the difficult Japanese language. Whenever he felt discouraged he would read over the poem and be motivated to work harder. Whether you find yourself feeling overwhelmed with the application process or with the workload of your upper level classes, remember that anything is possible if you are willing to work for it! Regardless of how you go about becoming a BYU Cougar, keep this poem in mind.

"Success" by Berton Braley

If you want a thing bad enough
To go out and fight for it,
Work day and night for it,
Give up your time and your peace and your sleep for it

If only desire of it
Makes you quite mad enough
Never to tire of it,
Makes you hold all other things tawdry and cheap for it

If life seems all empty and useless without it
And all that you scheme and you dream is about it

If gladly you'll sweat for it,
Fret for it,
Plan for it,
Lose all your terror of God or man for it

If you'll simply go after that thing that you want
With all your capacity,
Strength and sagacity,
Faith, hope and confidence, stern pertinacity

If neither cold poverty, famished and gaunt,
Nor sickness nor pain
Of body or brain
Can turn you away from the thing that you want,

If dogged and grim you besiege and beset it,
You'll get it![2]

---

[2] "Things as They Are, Ballads : Braley, Berton, B. 1882 : Free Download & Streaming." *Internet Archive.* Web. 28 February 2018. <https://archive.org/details/thingsastheyareb00bral>.

Applying as an Incoming Freshman

Each year, the average standardized test scores and GPA of incoming freshmen at BYU get more and more competitive. These high scores, coupled with an ever-increasing number of applicants, mean that getting accepted to BYU is a considerable achievement! Let's consider some of the 2017 fall incoming freshmen admission statistics.[3]

Applicants	Students Accepted	Average GPA	Average ACT/SAT	Acceptance Rate
13,707	7,317	3.86	29.5 / 1300	53.4%

In 2017, BYU's admission rate was 53.4%, compared to 64% in 2010 and 78% in 2005.[4] The average incoming freshman in 2017 had a solid 3.86 high school GPA. Of the 13,000 BYU applicants in 2016, a whopping 22% had perfect 4.0 high school GPAs and 54 applicants had perfect ACT scores. It's safe to assume that those numbers will continue to rise as BYU becomes even more competitive in the future.[5] These numbers highlight two basic things: BYU is a

---

[3] "Entrance Averages." *BYU Admissions*. Web. 12 February 2018. <https://admissions.byu.edu/entrance-averages>.

[4] Lenz, Sara. "Application Denied: Class of 2011 May Face Toughest Admission Competition Yet." *DeseretNews.com*. Deseret News, 27 Mar. 2011. Web. 28 February 2018. <http://www.deseretnews.com/article/700122163/Application-denied-Class-of-2011-may-face-toughest-admission-competition-yet.html>.

[5] Walch, Tad. "BYU Freshmen Averaged 29 on ACT, 1280 on SAT." *DeseretNews.com*. Deseret News, 07 Sept. 2016. Web. 28 February

tough school to get into, and it will only continue to get increasingly competitive.

GPA and ACT/SAT test scores are an important part of any aspiring Cougar's application package, but they aren't the only thing BYU will look at when considering you as an applicant. BYU also takes the following areas into consideration:

- Ecclesiastical endorsement
- Writing ability as demonstrated in the application essays
- Seminary attendance
- Service and leadership experiences
- Individual talents and creativity
- AP/IB courses taken
- Any other factors showing that you would be a strong asset to the BYU community[6]

It's a long list but making a conscious effort to improve yourself in these areas will pay dividends when applying to BYU.

If the long list of things to focus on is raising your stress level, consider the reason that BYU emphasizes them in the first place. Developing yourself in these areas will, in addition to making your application more competitive, help prepare you to be a more successful student. Take writing skill, for example: In addition to attracting the notice of BYU Admissions staff, students who can demonstrate a

---

2018<http://www.deseretnews.com/article/865661852/BYU-freshmen-averaged-29-on-ACT-1280-on-SAT.html>.

[6] "Acceptance Criteria." *BYU Admissions*. Web. 12 February 2018. <https://admissions.byu.edu/acceptance-application>.

high level of writing proficiency on their application essays will be at a huge advantage when assigned long or difficult writing assignments for their college courses. Regardless of your major, you will write many essays, analytical reports, and other papers at BYU, and if you are a weak writer, you will struggle with these assignments.

Think of it this way: *Writing well is important for your application because it is important for your success as a college student and as a future professional in your chosen field.* The other areas that BYU Admissions evaluates are equally important for your success as a student.

Applying as a Transfer Student
Let's look at the 2017 Fall semester transfer student admission statistics.[7]

Applicants	Students Accepted	Average GPA	Acceptance Rate
2,626	1,146	3.71	43.6%

As you can see, the acceptance rate for transfer students is lower than for new freshmen. However, the average GPA is also considerably lower. For students who had weak applications or were not accepted when applying as incoming freshman, applying as a transfer student is an excellent way to get into BYU and fulfil your dream of being a BYU Cougar.

---

[7] "Entrance Averages." *BYU Admissions*. Web. 28 February 2018. <https://admissions.byu.edu/entrance-averages>.

Students are eligible to apply to BYU as a transfer student providing they have 24 university-level class credits and have completed at least one university class after graduating from high school. Some students who are not initially accepted into BYU will choose to take university-level courses from another institution, through BYU Independent Study, or by attending BYU spring and summer terms as a visiting student until they have the 24 credit hours required to apply as a transfer student.

When applying to BYU as a transfer student, each applicant's college transcript is reviewed by BYU Transfer Evaluation Services to see which credits will transfer to BYU upon admission. Credits that usually transfer include credits from other accredited colleges and universities, credits earned at BYU while as a visiting student or night student, AP credits earned with an AP exam score of 3, 4 or 5, and IB credits achieved with a course score of 5, 6 or 7.[8] To see exactly what test scores are required to receive BYU credit refer to the AP/IB guide provided by the Registrar's office.[9]

The Foreign Language Achievement Testing Service (FLATS) is an excellent way for second-language speakers to quickly earn college credits that can count towards the BYU transfer application requirements.[10] The FLATS test allows any student, including non-BYU students, to take an exam and receive 12 foreign language credits for a nominal

---

[8] See "Transfer Credits." *BYU Admissions*. Web. 12 February 2018. <https://admissions.byu.edu/transfer-credits>, and "AP/IB Guides." *BYU Registrar's Office*. Web. 12 February 2018. <https://registrar.byu.edu/apib-guides>.

[9] https://registrar.byu.edu/apib-guides

[10] Humanities, Office Of Digital. *Foreign Language Achievement Testing Service*. Web. 28 February 2018. <https://flats.byu.edu/tips.php>.

fee. Students are restricted to taking FLATS tests for languages other than their native language.

BYU students, spring/summer visiting students, and BYU evening students also have the option to test out of 14 or 16 credits of language courses via the Challenge Exam.[11] Ben used the Challenge Exam to test out of 16 Japanese credits after returning from his mission in Tokyo. The 16 credits he earned combined with an additional 8 credits earned as a visiting student put Ben at 24 credits; he was able to apply to BYU as a transfer student and was accepted. For more information about the FLATS program and the Challenge Exam (see chapter 6: Speaking in Tongues).

If you don't already have at least 24 college credits, consider taking classes from another institution, from an online program, or at BYU as a spring/summer term visiting student. When considering what classes to take to get you to the 24-credit mark, taking classes that will transfer and fulfil general education requirements at BYU is a great idea. *Do whatever it takes to do extremely well in your classes.* Take your time and spread out your classes if necessary to ensure that you get the highest grades possible.

In addition to acing your classes to secure a strong GPA, work on developing your writing ability and service and leadership skills. High school GPA and ACT/SAT scores are not taken into consideration for transfer applicants with 24 or more college credits, so don't worry about retaking those tests if you did not do well the first time around.

If it is your dream to get into BYU, don't let anything get in your way. If acceptance as an incoming

---

[11] "Challenge & Exemption Exams." *BYU Registrar's Office*. Web. 28 February 2018<https://registrar.byu.edu/challenge-exemption-exams>.

freshman is not a reality for you, then follow the steps presented above to get accepted as a transfer student. It doesn't matter if you transferred into BYU or not; your diploma will be identical to the diploma earned by students who got into BYU as freshman!

Meet Your Admissions Representative

BYU has taken the initiative to pair each prospective student with an academic guidance counselor to whom they can turn with any admissions related questions or concerns. These men and women are intimately familiar with all the ins and outs of BYU's admission process and can help you get everything in order and submitted on time.

When Ben was applying as a transfer student, he found his admissions representative an incredibly valuable resource. Ben's admissions representative looked over his high school and college transcripts and advised Ben how to leverage his strengths during the application process, which eventually resulted in Ben being accepted to BYU as a transfer student. Visit BYU's admission representative webpage and get familiarized with your specific counselor.[12]

Take a Campus Tour

BYU has been nationally recognized for its excellent golf cart campus tours. These tours are a fantastic way for your whole family to get acquainted with BYU's beautiful, sprawling grounds. As reported in the *U.S. News & World Report*, "The golf cart tour has been commissioned to give the personalized tour to each family, showing the academic side of campus [. . .] Tour guides are 'BYU experts' who are

---

[12] "Admission Representatives." Admission Services, Web. 16 April 2018. <https://admissions.byu.edu/admission-representatives>.

'very personable, warm and gracious, and are wonderful at meeting the needs of prospective students.'"[13]

In addition to showing the campus, tours include information on the admissions process, academic departments, overall campus life, financial aid, scholarships, and extracurricular opportunities.[14] If you are in the area and would like to take a tour, check out the campus tours website. If you wish you could take a tour but can't get to campus, take advantage of a virtual campus tour!

Call to Action

Before moving on to chapter 2, we encourage you to do the following:

1. Visit the BYU admissions webpage[15] and familiarize yourself with all the important dates and deadlines that are applicable to you.

2. Sit down and conduct an in-depth evaluation of the strengths and weaknesses of each part of your application package. A great way to do this is to reread through the bulleted items on page 4 and rate yourself in each area.

3. Once finished, brainstorm ways you can improve, beginning with your weakest area first. Committing yourself to improving the weakest aspects of your

---

[13] Kern, Rebecca. "Colleges Attract Students With Unique Campus Tours." U.S. News & World Report, U.S. News & World Report, Web. 16 April 2018. <http://www.usnews.com/education/best-colleges/right-school/tours/articles/2010/04/08/colleges-attract-students-with-unique-campus-tours>.

[14] "Campus Tours." Admission Services, Web. 16 April 2018. <https://admissions.byu.edu/campus-tours>.

[15] https://admissions.byu.edu/admission-application

application could make the difference and help you get accepted!

4. Look up your admissions representative and contact them with any questions or concerns you have about the application process.

5. Consider scheduling one of BYU's fantastic golf cart campus tours.

CHAPTER TWO

Paying for School

Despite BYU's tuition only being about one fourth of the national average, paying for school can still be a challenge.[16] Luckily, each year thousands of students at BYU are awarded a variety of scholarships to help offset tuition, books, and even living expenses. In addition to academic and athletic scholarships, there is a wide variety of other scholarships available that many students are completely unaware of. This section will help you get an idea of the massive number of scholarships and grants available so that you can get in on the action!

FAFSA

The office of Federal Student Aid has provided a whopping $120 billion in federal need-based grants, merit-based scholarships and loans. Completing the Free Application for Federal Student Aid (FAFSA) form is the first step

---

[16] For the 2017-2018 academic year, the average price tag for a year's tuition at a private university in the United States was $21,419. Comparatively, BYU had a modest cost of only $5,460. See "2017 Tuition, Fees, and Living Costs Comparison Between Private Colleges (Undergraduate)." *College Tuition Compare*. Web. 12 February 2018. <http://www.collegetuitioncompare.com/compare/tables/?degree=Undergraduate&type=Private>.

in applying for a piece of that federal aid. In addition to being a necessary step when applying for federal aid, many nonfederal scholarships and secondary grants require applicants to have completed their FAFSA application. Hence, it is important that you complete your FAFSA application early. *A new FAFSA application must be completed each year.* For tips and guidance on completing your FAFSA and getting the most money possible, take some time to check out the U.S. Department of Education's Federal Student Aid webpage[17] as well as the BYU Financial Aid webpage.[18]

Federal Pell Grants

Pell Grants are provided by the federal government to students who complete a FAFSA application and meet specific need-based criteria. Federal Pell Grants are usually reserved for undergraduate students who have not yet earned a bachelor's or other professional degree. The best thing about these grants is that they are not loans and do not need to be repaid!

According to the U.S. Department of Education, the amount awarded to students will vary according to many factors, including your financial need, the cost of tuition, your status as a full- or part-time student, and whether you will be attending school for the full academic year. While the greatest possible amount awarded varies each year, the U.S. Department of Education reported that the maximum Pell Grant award possible for the 2017-2018 year was $5,920.[19] The average Pell Grant received by awardees is on the rise. In 2016-2017 students received an average Pell

---

[17] https://studentaid.ed.gov/sa/

[18] https://financialaid.byu.edu/federal-pell-grants

[19] "Federal Pell Grants." *Federal Student Aid.* 29 June 2017. Web. 12 February 2018. <https://studentaid.ed.gov/sa/types/grants-scholarships/pell>.

Grant of about $3,740.[20] Regardless of your financial situation, you should complete a FAFSA application each year.

Scholarships for Incoming Freshmen

Incoming freshmen are eligible for a variety of scholarships the first semester they enroll, including academic, minority, and need-based scholarships. The BYU Admission Services webpage states that each year, 50 freshmen will be awarded the full-tuition, multi-year Russell M. Nelson scholarship;[21] 200 freshmen will be awarded the full-tuition Heritage scholarship; 400 freshmen will receive one year of full tuition; and 1,000 incoming freshmen will be given one year of half tuition.[22]

For these academic scholarships, incoming freshmen are ranked according to their high school GPA and ACT/SAT scores. BYU awards these scholarships starting with the highest-ranked student first and awards scholarships down the line until all scholarships have been distributed.[23] All incoming freshmen are automatically considered for these scholarships and no extra action is required on the part of the student, assuming they have successfully submitted all required materials before the

---

[20] "Maximum and Average Pell Grants over Time." *Maximum and Average Pell Grants over Time - Trends in Higher Education - The College Board*. Web. 18 April 2018. <https://trends.collegeboard.org/student-aid/figures-tables/maximum-and-average-pell-grants-over-time>.

[21] The Presidential Scholarship is always named after the living Prophet/President of The Church of Jesus Christ of Latter-day Saints.

[22] "Scholarships." *BYU Admissions*. Web. 12 February 2018. <https://admissions.byu.edu/scholarships>.

[23] "View Scholarships FAQs." *OneStop Student Services*. Web. 12 February 2018. <https://onestop.byu.edu/view-scholarships-faqs#FAQ3>.

scholarship deadline.[24] Check the BYU Financial Aid webpage for more information.

Scholarships for Continuing Students

Continuing student academic scholarships are awarded to students who have completed at least 12 BYU credits by the end of the previous fall semester. BYU is composed of 10 colleges that each house several departments and dozens of majors and minors. Each college on campus awards the top students in the college with academic scholarships. Every college has its own GPA benchmarks used to determine which students will qualify for full- and half-tuition scholarships. These scholarships are very competitive, but focused, hard-working students can certainly position themselves to be the recipient of one of these prestigious scholarships for the entirety of their undergraduate career. Each student who meets the GPA benchmark set by their college will be awarded the appropriate academic scholarship provided they have filled out the appropriate forms in their BYU financial center and they meet the credit requirement.

Students who have not declared a major are also eligible for academic scholarships. These open majors are grouped together and compete against each other for academic scholarships as if they made up their own college. Be aware that open majors have some of the highest GPA requirements of any college on campus.

GPA requirements will fluctuate from year to year, but the 2017-2018 school year benchmarks should give you a good idea of the GPA needed to earn an academic scholarship. For the 2017-2018 school year, full-tuition scholarship GPA cutoffs ranged from 3.93 to 3.96 while half-tuition

---

[24] "New Freshman Scholarships." *BYU Financial Aid*. Web. 28 February 2018. <https://financialaid.byu.edu/new-freshman-scholarships>.

scholarship cutoffs ranged from 3.79 to 3.94, depending which college a student's major belonged to. For spring and summer term scholarships, all students who meet a specified cutoff will qualify for scholarship. For a 2018 spring and summer full-tuition scholarship, the required GPA for all students was 3.89 while the cutoff for half tuition was 3.65.[25] Check your college's webpage or contact your college's advisement center or the BYU Financial Aid office to find out what specific GPA cutoffs apply to you.

Athletic Scholarships

Sports scholarships are awarded to student athletes involved with one the university's sports programs. BYU reports awarding just over 250 student athlete scholarships with a combined worth of $4 million each year![26] While usually awarded to students who have been specifically recruited by the various sports organizations, it is possible for students to "walk on"[27] to a specific sports team and be awarded an athletic scholarship at the discretion of the coaching staff.

A great example of a successful walk-on athlete earning a scholarship is BYU alumnus Dennis Pitta, who joined the BYU football team in 2003. After working his way into a starting position, he became a key part of BYU's offense and was awarded All-American honors four times.

---

[25] "Former & Continuing Student Scholarships." *BYU Financial Aid.*. Web. 15 February 2018. <https://financialaid.byu.edu/former-continuing-student-scholarships>.

[26] *BYU Athletic Scholarships*. Web. 15 February 2018. <http://cougarclub.com/byu-athletic-scholarships>.

[27] *Walk on* refers to the practice of students attempting to join a sports team through a tryout or other vetting process rather than being recruited by coaches specifically to play as a scholarship athlete.

After a stellar career at BYU, Pitta was recruited by the Baltimore Ravens and won a Super Bowl ring in 2012.[28]

As a side note, different sports programs allocate their scholarships differently depending on the amount of funding they have available. For example, football, which usually has the most scholarship money of any sports program on campus, can offer a huge number of full tuition and partial tuition scholarships each year. On the other hand, smaller sports programs like baseball, golf, or volleyball may only have the equivalent of 10 or 15 full tuition scholarships available for distribution. These smaller programs have the flexibility to award their money as full tuition scholarships to a few athletes or as partial tuition scholarships split up between a larger number of athletes based on the needs of the program.

ROTC Scholarships

For students interested in military service, both the Army and Air Force Reserve Officer Training Corp (ROTC) programs are a fantastic way to begin their military service while also paying for school. The purpose of these programs is to train cadets to accept a commission and serve in the U.S. military after graduating. Recipients of an ROTC scholarship are typically awarded generous two-, three-, or four-year full-tuition scholarships (depending on how many years they need to complete their degree) and living sti-

---

[28] See "Dennis Pitta." *Wikipedia*. Wikimedia Foundation, 15 June 2017. Web. 28 February 2018. <https://en.wikipedia.org/wiki/Dennis_Pitta#College_career>. No doubt an important but generally unrecognized factor in Dennis Pitta's success on and off the field is the fact that Nate was his Resident Assistant at Stover Hall in Helaman Halls during Dennis's freshman year. It was probably in anticipatory gratitude that Dennis gave Nate one of Nate's favorite nicknames: *Naterade*.

pends that range from $300 a month for freshmen to $500 dollars a month for seniors.[29]

Cadets who accept an Army ROTC scholarship can expect to serve a four-year, full-time commitment with the Army or an eight-year, part-time service commitment with the Army National Guard. Air Force ROTC scholarship recipients can expect to serve four, six, or ten years of active duty with the Air Force as stipulated by their chosen specialty.[30] The Air Force ROTC Detachment 855 that serves BYU and University of Utah students further clarifies on its webpage: "Most officers' career fields incur a four-year commitment on active duty. Some career fields that require extensive follow-on training have a longer commitment. For instance, Pilots commit to serve ten years on active duty upon completion of pilot training, Combat Systems Officers commit to serve six years after completing training, and Air Battle Managers commit to serve for six years."[31]

Other Scholarships and Grants

Additionally, the Honors Department, Financial Center, Kennedy Center, and Office of Research and Creative Activities (ORCA) all have various merit-based scholarships and grants available to qualifying students. These scholarships and grants are oftentimes overlooked and sometimes even go unclaimed! Some of these scholar-

---

[29] "At a Glance." *Army.* Web. 15 February 2018. <https://marriottschool.byu.edu/army/about/at-a-glance/>, and "Home." *Air Force ROTC Detachment 855.* Web. 15 February 2018. <http://www.afrotcdet855.org/>.

[30] "Scholarships for Students & Enlisted Soldiers." *Goarmy.com.* Web. 15 February 2018. <http://m.goarmy.com/rotc/scholarships.m.html>, and "OVERVIEW." *U.S. Air Force ROTC - Scholarships Offered.* Web. 15 February 2018. <https://www.afrotc.com/scholarships>.

[31] "Frequently Asked Questions." *Air Force ROTC Detachment 855.* Web. 15 February 2018. <http://www.afrotcdet855.org/faq/>.

ships are worth more than $1,000 and could mean a huge payday for you. In 2012, Ben applied for and was awarded the Robert K. Thomas half-tuition scholarship through the Honors Department. That year, there were more Robert K. Thomas scholarships available than applicants, so everyone who took the time to apply was awarded a nice $1,250 paycheck!

The Honors Department also has information on some very prestigious national and international scholarships and awards. Scholarships like the Barry Goldwater Scholarship are awarded to highly qualified applicants and are valued at tens of thousands of dollars. Take some time to use the resources available to you at the Honors Department and see what scholarships are out there, but don't delay as you don't want to miss any application deadlines!

The Phi Kappa Phi chapter on campus, currently located in the Maeser building with the Honors Department, is another organization with different grants, scholarships, and awards available to qualified students. Phi Kappa Phi is a national honor society focused on "superior scholarship" and promoting excellence in others through personal achievement. Undergraduate students in the top 7.5% of their class are eligible for membership.[32] Phi Kappa Phi members can apply for a variety of awards on the Phi Kappa Phi webpage.[33]

The Financial Center on campus and the Financial Fitness Center webpage have lists of literally thousands of scholarships that you can apply for.[34] These scholarships

[32] "Phi Kappa Phi." *Eligibility | Phi Kappa Phi.* Web. 15 February 2018. <http://phikappaphi.byu.edu/content/eligibility>.

[33] "Highlight Your Membership." *The Honor Society of Phi Kappa Phi.* Web. 15 February 2018. <https://www.phikappaphi.org/>.

[34] https://financialaid.byu.edu/section/scholarships.

are offered by hundreds of different organizations across the country. Many of these scholarships have specific requirements, but if you meet those requirements, you could get a lot of money! With so many scholarships listed, there is a high likelihood that one or more will be a perfect fit for you.

For students interested in international study abroad programs and internships, the Kennedy Center has scholarships and financial aid packages available to qualifying students.[35] For a list of external scholarships, visit the Kennedy Center ISP scholarship webpage for even more ways to help fund your international study program.[36] Be sure to check with your college's advisement center as some colleges have programs available to help offset some of the cost of studying abroad.

The ORCA office awards $1,500 grants to students doing undergraduate research under the mentorship of a BYU professor or approved faculty member. Students applying for ORCA grants must complete a fairly rigorous application process that is usually due at the end of every October. Grant awardees are notified early the following year and are free to spend the $1,500 however they wish. Participation in the ORCA program is an awesome way to score some cash and get valuable one-on-one mentoring while designing and carrying out your own research project (see chapter 8: Undergraduate Research).

Fastweb, an online service that pairs students with millions of scholarships, is another source you can use to find and apply for scholarships and grants. Users simply fill

---

[35] "SCHOLARSHIPS AND FINANCIAL AID FOR INTERNATIONAL STUDY PROGRAMS." *Kennedy Center.* Web. 28 February 2018. <http://kennedy.BYU.edu/isp/financial-aid/>.

[36] http://kennedy.BYU.edu/ispscholarships/

out their profile, and the Fastweb service matches users with scholarships they are qualified for. Fastweb is an excellent way for you to get paired up with scholarships that match your specific strengths, interests, and skills.[37]

We hope you are starting to get an idea of just how many scholarships and grants are out there for the taking. With some work, you could significantly reduce or even eliminate the need for student loans and graduate from BYU debt-free. Do yourself a massive favor and take a few minutes to investigate the available options and apply to as many as you qualify for.

Surplus Scholarship Awards

BYU has crunched the numbers and calculated that for an LDS student, the cost of attending BYU for one year is roughly $19,000.[38] This number takes into consideration tuition, books, housing and food, transportation costs, and even a little spending cash. Based on the estimated total yearly cost of attendance, BYU students are eligible to receive a maximum of $19,000 of scholarship money from BYU each year. Scholarship recipients will have the first portion of their awarded money automatically applied to cover their tuition cost in their My Financial Center account. Any leftover scholarship money will then be deposited into the recipient's personal bank account.

Currently, a full year's tuition for an LDS student at BYU is a bit less than $6,000. This means that it is possible for you to get one or more BYU scholarships totaling up to $19,000 and, after tuition costs are deducted, have over

---

[37] "Scholarships for College Students, High School Seniors and Graduate Students."*Fastweb*. Web. 28 February 2018. <http://www.fastweb.com/>.

[38] "How Much Does It Cost?" *Admission Services*. Web. 01 May 2018. <https://admissions.byu.edu/how-much-does-it-cost>.

$13,000 deposited directly to your personal bank account. You can use this cash to cover miscellaneous school and living expenses, build up an emergency savings account, or even open a Roth IRA!

Talent Award Scholarships

In addition to the many athletic and academic scholarships, BYU awards scholarships to students with outstanding ability in art, athletics, communications, dance, design, music, and theatre and media arts. For application information see the scholarships webpage.[39]

Invest Some Time, Net Thousands in Cash

In *Smart Money Smart Kids,* personal finance guru Dave Ramsey and his daughter Rachel Cruze advise making scholarship applications a part-time job. They highlight the value of aggressively applying to any and all scholarships with a real-life example of a girl who was encouraged by her mother to fill out scholarship applications for an hour each day during her senior year of high school. Despite the drudgery of filling out the applications day after day, she ended up getting enough scholarships to pay for the first three years of college.[40]

In *The Daily Universe,* Madison McBride wrote an excellent article titled "BYU Students Underutilize Scholarship Opportunities."[41] McBride wrote, "BYU nursing

---

[39] "Scholarships." *Admission Services*, Web. 16 April 2018. <http://admissions.byu.edu/scholarships>.

[40] Ramsey, Dave, and Rachel Cruze. *Smart money smart kids: raising the next generation to win with money.* Brentwood, TN: Lampo Press, 2014. Print.

[41] McBride, Madison, Quincy Wilks, Joshua Ellis, and Kate Blood Ferguson. "BYU Students Underutilize Scholarship Opportunities." *The Daily Universe*. 03 Feb. 2016. Web. 28 February 2018. <http://universe.byu.edu/2016/02/03/byu-students-underutilize-scholarship-opportunities/>.

dent Bri Barnes has taken advantage of the scholarships offered at BYU. Barnes said she knew about scholarships but didn't realize how easy they would be to sign up for. She applied for a scholarship after her freshman year and said it only took her about five minutes. She was offered a full-tuition academic scholarship." Five minutes scored Bri a full-ride scholarship that is valued at over $5,000. That's equivalent to Bri making $60,000 an hour!

Yelena Bosovik is another amazing example of tenaciously applying for scholarships to pay the expensive tuition cost of her dream school. In an article she wrote titled "How I Did It: I applied for 100 College Scholarships," she shared that as a high school student, she "proceeded to hound my teachers, mentors and school administrators for letters of recommendation and leads for possible scholarships. And I prayed like crazy because I was determined to go to my private school of choice and a high price tag wasn't going to daunt me." She continued, "I thought of it this way—if I spent an hour filling out an application and got the funding, it would mean I'd made $250, $1,000 or even $10,000 an hour of free money. Not bad!"[42]

It doesn't matter if you are still in high school, are applying for college, or are about to start your senior year at BYU. Make time to find as many different scholarships and grants as possible and start applying like it is your job. Admittedly it's oftentimes boring, tedious work, but you will experience very few things in life that feel better than finding out you have been awarded a sizeable chunk of scholarship cash after a just few hours of work!

---

[42] Bosovik, Yelena. "I Applied for 100 College Scholarships." *LearnVest - Financial Planning Services and Personal Finance News.* 11 Sept. 2013. Web. 28 February 2018. <https://www.learnvest.com/2013/09/how-i-did-it-i-applied-for-100-college-scholarships/2/>.

Securing your scholarships early and not having to worry about finances will be a huge advantage to you as a student. Many students are constantly stressed with their finances or lack thereof. Many others are forced to work long hours to pay their way through school. BYU student Connor Peck sums it up perfectly as quoted in McBride's article: "My [Thomas S. Monson] scholarship has given me the ability and freedom to focus completely on school and not stress so much about finances."

Work Opportunities

It's an age-old question: Should you work while going to school? There are arguments to be had on both sides of the question, but we think that even students who don't need the money can still benefit from having a job that provides 10-20 hours of work per week.

Research shows that students with part-time jobs during the school year get better grades and in general do better as students throughout their undergraduate degree. Students who work a modest number of hours each week have better time management skills, which can correlate to an elevated GPA over their non-working peers. In fact, according to a report compiled at BYU, "students who work fewer than 15-20 hours often report higher GPAs than those who do not work at all.[43]

---

[43] See Dundes, Lauren, and Jeff Marx. "Balancing Work and Academics: Why Do Students Working 10 to 19 Hours Per Week Excel?" *College Student Retention* 8 (2006): 2-15. Web. 16 July 2017. <https://www.talent.wisc.edu/home/Portals/0/WiGrow/Balancing%20work%20and%20academics%20in%20college...pdf>, and Hammond, Shawn. "Effects of Employment on Student Academic Success." (2006): n. pag. Web. 16 July 2017. <http://www.byu.edu/hr/sites/default/files/effects_of_student_employment.pdf>., and Laskowski, Amy. "Working May Help Your GPA." BU Today, 30 Nov. 2009. Web. 28 February 2018. <https://www.bu.edu/today/2009/working-may-help-your-gpa/>.

In addition, you haven't gone to college to waste your time playing the days away. You're there first and foremost to prepare yourself for a professional career. There is no better way to prepare yourself for years of work than to put in years of work.

There are more benefits to working a job during your college years than just developing a good work ethic and earning money. Business professionals constantly rave about and engage in networking (see chapter 11: Networking). For the rest of us who aren't the meet-and-greet type, working in close association with professors, bosses, supervisors, and other students is a much more natural way of making professional connections that may lead to additional work opportunities, professional development, or perhaps a letter of recommendation to a future job or additional school.

Now that we've established some benefits of working during college, let's discuss some of the available resources.

On-Campus Employment

BYU employs thousands of students each year.[44] Since the majority of BYU students live within a mile or two of the campus, it's super convenient that there are so many jobs so close at hand. On-campus jobs can be related to your major or could be totally unrelated, such as custodial work or selling Cougar Tails at the concession stand during football games.

Many on-campus internships will be unpaid for at least the first semester, but if you get in and prove yourself a good worker, often those unpaid gigs that you needed an-

---

[44] About 16,000, according to the BYU Student Employment Office. They said they have "backroom reports" but that there are no actual statistics published for general consumption anywhere.

yway for your major can turn into longer-term paid positions.

Nate, for instance, started out as an unpaid undergraduate intern at the on-campus wellness clinic Y-Be-Fit. He continued working there for pay for the rest of his undergraduate degree and ultimately became one of the two graduate co-directors for the first two years of his master's degree.

Ben, on the other hand, taught Japanese at the Missionary Training Center (MTC), where he was able to use his mission language to help his students prepare to serve the Japanese people—while also making enough to pay for rent and food. These are just two of the many on-campus jobs we held during our time at BYU. The possibilities and opportunities are almost endless.

In the Wilkinson Student Center (WILK) you will find the Student Employment office. Every open position on campus is listed there. If you need a job and want to work on campus, all you need to do is visit the Student Employment office or check out its website,[45] and you will likely have a job secured before long.

Whether you apply online or in person for an on-campus job, you're going to need to complete an I-9 certification to complete the hiring process. A United States passport or a driver's license and a Social Security card are required to complete the I-9, so you'll want to have those with you. Check out the Student Employment office website for more examples of acceptable forms of identification.[46]

---

[45] http://www.byu.edu/hr/?q=student-jobs

[46] "Human Resource Services." *What Do I Need to Get Hired?* Web. 28 February 2018. <http://www.byu.edu/hr/?q=student-jobs%2Ffaq-working-campus%2Fwhat-do-i-need-get-hired>.

Off-Campus Employment

We've talked about on-campus employment, but what about off-campus jobs? There are tons of those too! The best thing about getting out into the community to work is that those are often the kinds of jobs that can lead to long-term employment after graduation.

Now, you may not want to stick around in Provo for the rest of your life, but when you are working an off-campus job—especially if it's related to your major—you are out in the so-called *real world*, with real supervisors and real responsibilities that can very easily translate into finding the kind of job you want after you graduate.

Very few, if any, of you will have a professor approach you on the day of your graduation and say that he or she wants to employ you for the kind of wages you hope to earn once you've finished your degree. But off-campus employers can do just that. They've seen you work, they've come to appreciate what you have to offer their company, and they want you to continue being a part of it.

If you want to move to another part of the country or world, your employer can often connect you to old friends and colleagues or at least write you a strong letter of recommendation to help you secure employment wherever you go. It's definitely worth looking into, especially as you get into your junior and senior year of school.

Start a Business

Another way to earn money and gain real-world experience is to start your own business while in college. You'd be surprised what skills and talents you have that are highly marketable. And one of the big plusses of starting your own business is that you can set your own hours and be your own boss.

If you speak a foreign language or are good at math or writing, you could tutor middle school, high school, and even fellow university students. You could certify to be a personal trainer and drum up clients to train. Perhaps you did a lot of custodial work growing up. You could get a few gigs cleaning local office buildings in the early mornings or later in the evening. Or maybe you enjoy building websites. You could find some smaller local businesses that desperately need a good website, or you could build sites to sell online to interested parties.

Several BYU students have created insanely successful apps that have helped pay for school as well as made them very rich! For example, in 2015 Garrett Gee and his team sold their app The Scan, Inc., to Snapchat for a cool $54 million![47] Again, the possibilities are endless. All you need is an idea, the willingness to work, and a few available hours each week.

While he never made close to the $54 million bucks that Gee made, Ben did start his own business as a personal trainer while a student at BYU. Ben was fortunate enough to be hired as a personal trainer at a small gym working with a good friend and former mission companion. After about two years working at the gym, Ben set off on his own with the hopes of training groups of people at various small businesses around Utah Valley. He helped several businesses select gym equipment and build small gyms in their warehouses and offices. Training mostly early in the mornings, Ben worked with dozens of people and earned enough money to graduate from BYU with zero student loan debt. As a side note, Ben was also able to make many meaningful relationships with his clients that included lawyers, a PA, a nurse, many small business owners, and a partner at a pres-

[47] Crofts, Lisa, Nastassja Krupczynski, Savannah Ius, and Katelyn Kenedy. "BYU Student Sells App to Snapchat for $54 Million." *The Daily Universe*. 22 June 2015. Web. 28 February 2018. <http://universe.byu.edu/2015/06/22/byu-student-sells-app-to-snapchat-for-54-million11/>.

tigious capital investment firm. Through these relationships, Ben was introduced to a variety of doctors he shadowed and from whom he secured several strong letters of recommendation in preparation for medical school.

Which brings us to another important point: Most students will have the time to work 10-20 hours every single week for every semester of their undergraduate degree. Whether you do paid (jobs and some internships) or unpaid (internships and service) work, you should plan on scheduling 10-20 hours of work for every single week during your undergraduate degree. It really is that important to your success as a student—working students on average do better than non-working students, remember?—and as a future professional.

Summers and Breaks

Most students will not go to school literally year-round (although that's also an option—one that we both capitalized on during our time at BYU). If you aren't going to school during the summer months, or if you take a winter semester off so that you can get out of Provo during the winter, you should find yourself a job or internship that will give you at least 40 paid hours per week. Not only will you earn money (which will help pay for your next semesters if you don't have scholarships or grants), but you have a dedicated three months to really dive into the workforce and better prepare yourself for your post-graduation transition from being a student to being a working professional. These are not months to be squandered on playing and frivolity. There will be plenty of fun times even if you are holding down a full-time job or internship during your break. The summer is also a great time to snag that job you have had your eye on as most students will leave campus over the summer and quit their on-campus jobs. Summer time is a great chance for you to level up jobs and score those higher paying positions as well.

Call to Action

We highly recommend that after reading through this chapter a couple of times, you develop a plan to help you meet your financial goals.

1. Decide how much time each day you are going to devote to finding and applying to scholarships and make that time a special priority!
2. Analyze your school schedule and decide if a part-time job is right for you. If you plan to find a job, set aside time each day to apply for work.
3. If your resume could use some sprucing up, check out the University Career Services webpage[48] for some excellent tips!

---

[48] "University Career Services." *Resume | University Career Services*. Web. 28 February 2018. <https://careers.byu.edu/search/?s=resume>.

CHAPTER THREE

Majors, Minors, Etc.

Picking a Major/Minor

What do you want to be when you grow up? How many times have you heard that throughout your life? Probably too many to count. And yet here you are at college. You're at the brink of full-fledged adulthood with your whole life ahead of you. There's much riding on the decisions you make in these few short years regarding what degree program to pursue.[49]

No pressure or anything, right?

While it's true that the next decade of your life—often called the decade of decision—is critically important, it's also not something to freak out about. There are a ton of resources available to you at BYU to help you navigate the myriad options that lay before you. This chapter will help you connect to some of them. We very highly recommend you visit the BYU University Advisement Center and any of

---

[49] "University Advisement Center." *Things To Consider When Choosing A Major | University Advisement Center*. University Advisement Center, Web. 28 February 2018.
<https://universityadvisement.byu.edu/node/74>.

the specific college advisement centers that correspond to the departments that house the majors and minors you're most interested in for even more resources than we can mention here.

To Those Who Know

Maybe you are one of those lucky ones who has always known what you want to be in your professional career. In which case, congratulations! Go declare your major and get to work. (But don't toss this book aside, because there's still a lot in it for you.)

To Those Who Don't

If you're anything like Nate was (and, to an extent, still is), then you have spent many hours agonizing over the implications of answering the question of what to major in once and for all and choosing one path to the exclusion of the rest.

You may be one who enjoys learning for learning's sake and struggles with the idea of choosing just one thing to study and sticking to it for life. You're not a pigeon, and you don't like being pigeon-holed.

While you are bound to suffer more in the major-picking process than your fellows who are laser-focused on being accountants or nurses or engineers, there's no need to abandon all hope. There are some really good resources available to help you navigate the fraught waters of choosing a program of study.

What Do You Like and What Are You Good At?

If you've never taken a Career Interest Survey before, then it's time you head down to the Academic Success Center in room 2590 WSC to meet with the lovely people there who will help you get to know yourself better.[50] There

---

[50] https://casc.BYU.edu/

are two surveys that you can take for free online and another three that are available in 2590 WSC for a small fee.[51]

Nate took one such survey in high school and learned that he should join the clergy. Not very helpful for a Latter-day Saint. What he should have done after his mission—but, alas!, didn't—was take one or more similar surveys to see what was really up.

BYU also offers some great student development classes to help you navigate this process of figuring out what to study and what career to pursue after graduation.[52] If you are at BYU but don't really know what you want to study or what kind of job you want after you graduate, student development courses could be your pathway to major and career enlightenment.

One of the best resources available to you beside the University Advisement Center and the various college advisement centers for assessing the future job market is the US Bureau of Labor Statistics Occupational Outlook Handbook.[53]

Of course, many, many people have made great careers for themselves in fields unrelated to their major. But feeling like you may have chosen the wrong major and wasted all those years in college is very real.

---

[51] Between $10 and $16.

[52] The full list of Student Development Courses is available on the Academic Success Center website," University Advisement Center." *Student Development Classes | University Advisement Center*. Student Development Classes, Web. 28 February 2018. <https://universityadvisement.byu.edu/student-development-classes>.

[53] Check out the United States Department of Labor website, "Home : Occupational Outlook Handbook:." *U.S. Bureau of Labor Statistics*. U.S. Bureau of Labor Statistics, Web. 28 February 2018. <https://www.bls.gov/ooh/home.htm>.

A little preparation and forethought—not to mention applying the principles we outline in this book—will help you avoid some of the pitfalls we've experienced ourselves and seen in others' experiences.

Majors

A major can be anywhere from about 45 to 100 credits in length, give or take.[54] In other words, your major takes up the majority of your undergraduate credits.[55] The rest is mostly general education credits and other electives (read: The perfect spot for a minor or two).

Every major is going to have its bad side(s), so don't avoid a major simply because you hear it's hard, or professor so-and-so isn't nice, or whatever it is that kids are saying these days.

Your major should be something you are genuinely interested in. If not, then there'll be nothing to keep you there when you're sick of it and want to quit—almost everyone experiences those feelings at least once during their program of study. It should be something that uses your talents and develops new ones too. And it should be something that can support you financially once you've graduated.

For those of you who agonize over what you should major in, remember that there probably isn't just one major that you absolutely have to pursue or you'll never fulfill your life's mission. Start by getting a feel of what sorts of

---

[54] In our unscientific study of the hundreds of majors BYU offers, we saw one degree as low as 41 credits and another as high as 103.5 credits. We didn't look at every major, but we think you now have a decent idea of what to expect from your major by way of length or size.

[55] Except for when it doesn't, as is the case for any major that is less than 61 credit hours in length.

majors are available by looking at the complete list of currently offered BYU majors on the BYU website.[56]

We hear a lot about personal missions in life, and it can seem as if our career decisions factor heavily into whether we will accomplish those personal missions or not. This may be the case for a small number of us, but we suggest that whatever we have by way of a personal mission in life, it likely doesn't hinge exclusively on what career we pursue. There are many statements by many prophets and apostles to the effect that the Lord doesn't care what we do for a living as long as it's honorable.[57]

Minors: No Small Thing (Sometimes)

Minors—comprised of a cluster of related courses— are usually smaller than majors, falling between 13 and 42 credit hours in length.[58] There are more than 100 minors to choose from.[59] You might want to choose one or two cognate minors that pair well with and complement your major, such as nutrition to exercise science, or editing to

---

[56] https://catalog.byu.edu/majors

[57] President Hinckley, for example, Hinckley, Gordon B. "A Prophet's Counsel and Prayer for Youth." *Ensign Jan. 2001 - Ensign.* Web. 15 July 2017. <https://www.lds.org/ensign/2001/01/a-prophets-counsel-and-prayer-for-youth?lang=eng>. When President Hinckley gave this talk on 12 November 2000, Nate was in attendance in BYU's Marriott Center. It was a powerfully spiritual experience.

[58] Again, we very unscientifically studied the just over one hundred minors BYU offers. We saw one minor as low as 13 credits and another as high as 42 credits. We didn't look at every minor, but we think you now have a decent idea of what to expect from the minors by way of length or size.

[59] "Minors." *Undergraduate Catalog.* Web. 28 February 2018. <https://catalog.byu.edu/minors>.

English. Or you might be a pre-med student[60] and have to take so much chemistry that you may as well take the last one or two courses to complete the minor. (Ben did exactly that.) You might choose some subject that you've always loved, want to get better at, and would like to do for the rest of your life but don't necessarily see yourself majoring in, like dance.

For all you science, technology, engineering and math (STEM) majors, adding a humanities minor is a perfect way to help you expand the breadth of your education, gain exposure to different ways of thinking, improve your writing skills, and learn to view arguments from a different perspective.

For exactly these same reasons, it is invaluable for humanities majors to add some sort of STEM minor. In fact, Humanities+, a program sponsored by the College of Humanities, is entirely devoted to helping students understand the benefits of and get involved with outside disciplines for a broader, more comprehensive education.[61]

Whatever the reason for choosing one or more minors, it's a good reason as long as doing so doesn't unnecessarily delay graduation. Minors can add breadth to your studies or teach you new skills that will come in handy when you face a career change later on in life, and odds are that you will face at least one career change in your life.

---

[60] There is no "pre-med" major at BYU, per se, but if you want to attend medical school, you can fit in the prerequisite courses into any major you want. If this is your plan, make sure you go to the Pre-Professional Advisement Center (https://ppa.BYU.edu/) as soon as possible to get onto the right track.

[61] "Humanities+." *BYU Humanities*. Web. 28 February 2018. <http://humanities.BYU.edu/about-the-college/humanitiesplus/>.

Since an undergraduate degree is a minimum of 120 credits, all it will take to get a minor is some discipline to organize your coursework early. You don't want to accumulate a bunch of random classes and credits that fulfill little more than your curiosity.

Double Major

It's not very often that you hear of someone double majoring, but it does happen and is a good option for some students. If you are considering adding a second major, be aware that there is a petition form that must be submitted to the Registrar's office. Also, it is critical that students petition to add a second major *before* they hit 75 BYU credits, not counting language exam credits.[62] Having a second major is an involved process, so be sure to start the process early.

Honors Program

The Honors Program is neither a major nor a minor, but it is a fabulous way for you to enrich your undergraduate studies by participating in intellectually diverse and challenging coursework, an original research project, and the Great Questions Essay (see chapter 4: Honors Program).

Religious Education

As you are no doubt well aware, BYU's sponsoring institution is The Church of Jesus Christ of Latter-day Saints. The Church provides religious education for its young adult membership between the ages of 18 to 30 years through its Institute program. In lieu of attending Institute classes in addition to one's coursework as at non-LDS universities, BYU students have their religious education courses built into their academic programs.

---

[62] See "Petition to Add a Second Major." BYU Registrar's Office, https://registrar.BYU.edu/advisement/forms/second_major.pdf>.

It is a truth universally acknowledged that the hope of nearly every returned missionary is to enroll or reenroll at BYU, major in religion, and continue his or her mission indefinitely.[63] Well, not exactly, but we've met returned missionaries who seemed to hope that such an option was available. We can't blame them either: Nate chose to attend BYU specifically because it requires religion courses for graduation.

The truth is that there are no religion-focused majors at BYU that might be found at other universities, which may seem odd given BYU's status as a church-sponsored university. We don't know exactly why this is the case and we don't intend on speculating either.

If your heart is set on eventually becoming a professor of religious studies or church history or something along those lines, you'll need to major in some other undergraduate degree at BYU—like history, or ancient Middle Eastern studies, or classical studies with an emphasis on ancient Greek—and then ultimately attend some other university for graduate studies.

There are also no minors, per se, offered through the college of Religious Education, but every BYU graduate will have roughly the equivalent of a minor once all religion courses are accounted for (14 credit hours).

Despite not offering any undergraduate majors or minors in religion (though Family History - Genealogy comes close, given its importance in Latter-day Saint theology and praxis), the Department of Religious Education does offer Seminary/Institute Preservice Training to allow students to explore a career within the Church Education System (CES). The preservice training consists of two

---

[63] We offer our deepest apologies to the late, great Jane Austen for our tawdry misuse of her classic opening line.

courses, Teaching Seminary (Rel 471) and Seminary Teaching Seminar (Rel 475), and can be integrated into any course of study.[64]

There's nothing stopping you from taking as many religion courses as you want. However, be careful: By taking more religion classes than are required for graduation, you will be earning extra credits that could be going to an actual minor, or you could be spending time and money that isn't getting you closer to graduation.[65]

The costs and benefits of taking extra religion courses must be calculated individually, as it is a personal decision, and we recognize that the religion courses are part of what makes BYU special among universities.

Declare a Major, Help Your Scholarship Chances
Maybe you came to BYU with one of its many scholarships, and maybe you didn't. In either case, once you've earned 12 BYU credits as a "day continuing student," you can qualify for a Former and Continuing Student Scholarship.[66] But you must meet pretty stringent cumulative GPA cutoffs.

Note: If you have not declared a major, the GPA cutoffs to receive one of these scholarships during the regular school year (fall and winter semesters) are 3.95 for full LDS tuition and 3.87 for half LDS tuition, which are higher

---

[64] https://religion.byu.edu/questions-and-policies
[65] Local Institute classes are a great place for you to continue a comprehensive study of the scriptures and teachings of modern-day prophets without incurring a lot of extra cost or homework assignments.

[66] "Former & Continuing Student Scholarships." *BYU Financial Aid.* Web. 15 February 2018. <https://financialaid.byu.edu/former-continuing-student-scholarships>.

cutoffs than are found in every BYU college except one: Nursing.[67]

Notice, too, that if you'll stick around for spring and summer terms, the GPA cutoffs to receive scholarships drop compared to the regular school year cutoffs for most colleges with a full tuition scholarship requiring a 3.89 GPA and half tuition scholarships needing a 3.65 (see chapter 2: Paying for School - Athletic Scholarships). Taken together, spring and summer terms add up to a regular semester, and you could take off the winter semesters to escape to somewhere warm for an internship or study abroad.

Before you commit to such a course, however, you'll want to make sure that by doing so you aren't disrupting your timeline to graduation. Certain upper-division courses are often taught in winter semesters only and sometimes only every other year. If you have one of those types of classes in your program, you don't want to miss it!

Extra Credits

Entering freshmen often come to BYU with college credit before they've even taken a single BYU class. It could be from Advanced Placement (AP) or International Baccalaureate courses or dual enrollment programs that a lot of high schools offer through a local community college or university. Some new freshmen can even be halfway finished with their freshman year (15 credits completed), maybe even into their sophomore year (30 credits completed) before school has even started. Nate knew of someone who had an incredible 54 credits under his belt coming out

---

[67] Ibid. That is, for the fall/winter 2017-2018 semesters. We imagine the numbers might change from year to year, but that the same general trend will continue. As near as we can tell, the BYU Nursing program is one of the most competitive and prestigious programs offered. Thus, it's not surprising at all that the Nursing program would have such high GPA cutoffs for scholarships.

of high school, all from AP tests. He was almost a credit junior as an entering freshman!

We encourage you to not assume that because the college credit you've earned fulfills the equivalent of key GE courses that you should skip over them entirely once you're at BYU. We feel it's better to take the equivalent honors class or the next-level course to be sure you truly develop the university-level skill set that is so important for the rest of your college career and beyond.

Of course, if your AP credits cover General Education credits (GEs) in departments that are completely unrelated to your degree or are not critical to your development as a university student, then by all means go your way rejoicing over time well spent in your high school years getting yourself ahead of the game.

Shadow

One of the best ways to learn whether you want to go into a particular field of study and into a subsequent career is to interview and shadow someone who currently works in the field you're interested in. Nate, for instance, had the romantic notion that he wanted to become a university professor because he really enjoyed teaching. He got a master's degree and applied for and was accepted into a PhD program.

All was going well until he came to the realization that being a professor wasn't at all like he had imagined. For some reason, despite the fact that he was in almost constant contact with a host of professors during his undergraduate and two graduate programs, Nate never really sat down with a single one to talk about what it's really like to work in academia with its demanding teaching *and* research schedule, publish-or-perish process of gaining tenure, myriad conferences to attend, often cutthroat intradepartment politics, stress of applying for and securing grant monies, and more.

How different his academic and career trajectories might have been if Nate had had the forethought to see what it would really be like working in the ivory tower. He could have studied the exact same fields, but had he known better that academia wasn't a great fit for him, he could have focused his energies on internships and other work experiences that would have been a better use of his time than the heap of teaching he did without getting a teaching degree or certificate. (Who wants to be adjunct faculty for life because you didn't get a PhD?)

Economic Viability

While it is undeniably important to study something you enjoy, it's just as important to keep an eye on the specific types of jobs that your studies could lead to and on their expected growth in future years.

As you can imagine, once the automobile became a popular consumer item, graduates in programs of horse breeding and buggy and wagon manufacture were probably kicking themselves for studying something that was soon to become obsolete. Let's hope they quickly retooled and got into an automotive design division at a car and truck company.

So how do you see into the future when it comes to potential jobs? Well, seeing into the future is technically impossible as far as we humans are concerned—shy of a major revelation—but we do have our ways of looking at past trends and the current job market and using those numbers to forecast what the future might look like.

Speaking with a career counselor or looking at the relevant statistics and forecasts[68] will help you make an in-

---

[68] The United States Department of Labor, for instance, publishes a very helpful guide, "The Occupational Outlook Handbook," that can tell you almost all you need to know about the jobs you're most interested in. See "Home : Occupational Outlook Handbook:." *U.S. Bureau of Labor Sta-*

formed decision so as to minimize the likelihood of getting yourself into a situation where you're graduating and then entering into a supersaturated job market or into a field that's become obsolete. Good, hard data out there can give you an idea for the prospects in your chosen field of study.

As a general rule, for example, there are more people graduating with PhDs these days in the U.S. than there are positions requiring PhDs, [69] making it difficult to get a job that matches level of education or is even in the same or related field of study.

A little homework into the economic viability of your intended course of study before you commit a lot of time and money—often with interest—to getting your degree will pay dividends in the end. And be sure to check out chapter 2: Paying for School for lots of great ways to avoid the whole debt with interest issue in the first place.

Call to Action

1. If you haven't already declared a major and have no idea what you want to study or what type of career you'd like to pursue, visit the Academic Success Center and avail yourself of their services.
2. If you've narrowed down your major (or minor) choices to a few solid options, make appointments to visit the specific college advisement centers to gather more information.

---

tistics. U.S. Bureau of Labor Statistics, Web. 28 February 2018. <https://www.bls.gov/ooh/>.

[69] This is illustrated in an April 2016 article by McKenna, Laura. "The Ever-Tightening Job Market for Ph.D.s." *The Atlantic.* Atlantic Media Company, 21 Apr. 2016. Web. 28 February 2018. <https://www.theatlantic.com/education/archive/2016/04/bad-job-market-phds/479205/>.

3. Visit the U.S. Bureau of Labor Statistics website for the Occupational Outlook Handbook to "comparison shop" for jobs related to your chosen major or for the majors you are seriously considering. Make a point to note the level of education required for the jobs, the median pay, and the projected growth rates.

CHAPTER FOUR

Honors Program

University Honors

The designation *University Honors* is the highest distinction BYU awards its graduates, and it is sometimes referred to as "highest honors." Only about 4,100 young men and women have graduated with Honors since the program was begun 47 years ago.[70] While every BYU student is eligible to participate in the Honors Program and graduate with Honors if they meet the requirements, each year, on average, fewer than 100 of over 8,000 undergraduate students will earn the distinction of graduating with Honors. That means that students graduating with Honors make up roughly just 1% of all undergraduates who earn their degrees each year.

Preparation for Graduate Programs

The knowledge and skills gained through the rigorous academic scholarship required by the Honors Program will help prepare you for any graduate level programs you may be considering after you graduate from BYU. The

---

[70] "BYU Honors." *History of the Honors Program (Our Story) | BYU Honors.* Web. 28 February 2018. <http://honors.byu.edu/content/history-honors-program>.

Honors Program coursework is designed to teach students how to perform top-tier research, write articulate and well-researched papers, and think critically. By mastering these skills during your undergrad, you will have a significant head start in your upper-level courses, and your transition into upper-level academia will be smoother.

Not Just an Accolade

Graduating with Honors is much more than just an opportunity to set yourself apart from your peers and get a cool distinction on your transcript. Rather, participating in the Honors Program is a wonderful way for you to enrich your undergraduate years as you engage in interdisciplinary study, develop a broader knowledge base, and increase your scholastic prowess.

Involvement in the Honors Program will also introduce you to other students who are as creative, motivated, and passionate as you are about learning and scholarship. As you mingle with them, you will be exposed to new ideas that will help shape how you think and perceive the world around you.

Ben credits several of his Honors classes for catalyzing his transformation from someone just putting in the time to earn a degree into someone eager to learn. The exposure to differing viewpoints in his Honors classes helped him shed some of his long-held misconceptions and unsubstantiated opinions. On the opposite side of the same coin, other opinions and beliefs were validated and strengthened as they held up through rigorous scrutiny and examination. While you progress through the Honors Program, you will similarly develop the critical thinking skills that will benefit you for the rest of your life.

Required Coursework

The Honors Program is constantly being updated and improved upon to ensure that it "better prepares students for the demands they will face in their post baccalaureate careers."[71] The current requirements for graduating with Honors include taking 14 hours of Honors coursework, completing an experiential learning experience or study abroad experience, engaging in a meaningful mentored research project (many students will kill two birds with one stone and use their Honors Thesis as an ORCA project, capstone, or part of an undergraduate research project) followed by a thesis defense, and completing the Great Questions Essay.

The required coursework includes several interdisciplinary courses with an emphasis on helping students become better scholars. One of the best aspects of these courses is that they will introduce you to viewpoints or ways of thinking that you may have never considered before. You will get to see how the other side of an argument views and thinks about things. Some of these classes are taught by two professors, each having different specialties and backgrounds so that you can study a subject from two different points of view.

Many of the classes that make up the required coursework for Honors students are designed specifically for "challenging students to think open-mindedly and to overcome ingrained paradigms of thinking," all while fulfilling university general education requirements.[72]

Experiential Learning

In fulfilling the experiential learning requirement, students must participate in an approved, education-related service, an international program like study abroad, or the honors peer mentoring program.

---

[71] "BYU Honors." *Frequently Asked Questions | BYU Honors*. Web. 28 February 2018. <http://honors.byu.edu/faq#different>.

[72] "BYU Honors." *Course Information | BYU Honors*. Web. 28 February 2018. <http://honors.byu.edu/course-information>.

Students can fulfill the experiential learning requirement by participating in service projects such as tutoring through the Y-Serve program, assisting the accessibility center,[73] or working with a non-profit organization. Students are also free to work with the Honors Department and design a project of their own.

Students can also engage in one of several different internship programs. These programs consist of various university-sponsored studies abroad, field-studies, and international internships (see chapter 9: Internships).

The last option that fulfills the experiential learning requirement is to participate in the Honors Students Advisory Council or Honors Peer Mentoring Program as a teaching assistant. This is an excellent way to get some quality leadership experience (see chapter 14: Student Council).

Honors Thesis and Thesis Defense
The Honors Thesis is a significant research project and an opportunity for students to engage in original research while being mentored by a consulting professor of the student's choosing. Students will typically plan and carry out research relating to their major or minor. Ben, who majored in Japanese, decided to focus his Honors Thesis on the difference between different foreign language studying methods with the hope of discovering the most effective way to study a foreign language and successfully store the newly studied information in long-term memory.[74] To help you get a further idea of what types of research students are

---

[73] "University Accessibility Center." *University Accessibility Center*. Web. 28 February 2018. <https://uac.byu.edu/>.

[74] Black, Benjamin R. *The Impact of Different Learning Styles on Language Study and the Formation of Long Term Memory*. Provo: Brigham Young U, 2016. Print.

doing for their theses, some other completed Honors Thesis topics include: *Tumor-Associated Macrophages: Ally or Enemy* by Heather M. Aamodt (2005), *Book Cover Illustration of the Classics* by John D. Adams (1996), *Dress and Ornament in the Works of Jane Austen by Heather B. Cook (2002),* and *Russian Oil and U.S. Foreign Policy in the Middle East* by Paul M. Cox (2003).[75]

After finishing your research and writing your thesis, you will defend your thesis in front of a panel of faculty composed of your thesis advisor, a faculty reader who is familiar with your project, and an Honors Coordinator.[76] After you present an overview of your project, including methodology, a summary of any data gathered, and final conclusions the panel will ask questions and make suggestions. The advisory panel will either declare the project successfully completed or will suggest things that need to be fixed before the thesis is completed.

Your completed Honors Thesis will be bound and housed within the Honors Thesis collection in the Harold B. Lee Library. A copy of each thesis is also available in the originating academic department and in an online archive.

Great Questions Essay

In addition to the coursework, experiential learning, and thesis, you will complete the Great Questions Essay. A relatively new requirement, the Great Questions Essay is a 15-20 page paper written on a topic of your choice and is much broader in scope than the thesis. When brainstorming topics for their Great Questions Essay, students are encouraged to contemplate the important questions that

---

[75] "BYU Honors." *Thesis Archive | BYU Honors*. Web. 28 February 2018. <http://honors.byu.edu/content/thesis-archive>.

[76] "BYU Honors." *Thesis Overview | BYU Honors*. Web. 28 February 2018. <http://honors.byu.edu/content/thesis-overview>.

matter most to themselves. A broad range of disciplines and resources should be used to answer the question. The Honors Department further explains the idea behind the Great Questions Essay on its website:

> "Questions, not answers, drive us. We know that questions are the driving force behind true education. As education advances, so does an ever-broadening chain of questions about why and how things work the way they do, what is or should be important to us, and, above all, what can or should be done about the problems and concerns we face in our collective and individual lives. We believe that no single discipline has the ability to provide us the answers to the questions that we have. All disciplines are important to solving and answering the great questions that face us in the world today. Here at BYU, this is especially pertinent due to our quest for knowledge through both the intellect and the spirit."[77]

To get their Great Questions Essay off to the right start, Honors students are required to enroll in HONRS 310 - Great Questions Tutorial, so don't worry if you are having a little trouble at first coming up with the perfect question to write your essay about.

Honors Advisement Newsletter

Another awesome resource provided by the Honors Department is a weekly newsletter that is emailed to Hon-

---

[77] "BYU Honors." *What Great Questions Drive You? | BYU Honors*. Web. 28 February 2018. <http://honors.byu.edu/what-great-questions-drive-you-0>.

ors students. It contains tons of information about keynote speakers who will be speaking at BYU over the coming week, information about Honors Department socials and other friendly gatherings, the famous "chocolate milk discussions" where students can sit and talk with professors while enjoying BYU's delicious chocolate milk, get helpful tips about upcoming graduation and career fairs, and more.[78] This newsletter is unbelievably convenient and helpful for keeping track of all the things going on that are otherwise easy to miss.

Though Ben was involved with an older version of the Honors Program, he can attest to the value it added to both his experience as a BYU student and to his life as a whole. It was awesome to have the distinction of being part of just 1% of BYU students who graduate with Honors, but more than that, his involvement with the Honors Program helped him begin to look at the world through a broader and clearer lens. Through the Honors Program, he became more objective in his decision making, and his experiences taught him to do a better job of considering both sides of an issue before making his own decisions and adopting his own opinions. Being astute and discerning when considering an issue is a priceless ability in today's world where facts are often skewed or downright falsified in an attempt to get as many clicks or views as possible.

Call to Action
Graduating with Honors does require a serious time commitment, but spread out over several years, it is doable for even the busiest students. At the end of the day, you won't regret the extra time spent pursuing a deeper level of scholarship while the opportunity is available to you. The following list will get you started.

---

[78] Some say the cookies 'n creme milk is even better!

1. Browse the Honors Department website for additional information.
2. Take a look at the course catalogue for the upcoming semester, paying special attention to the Honors classes that interest you. If you are unsure if the Honors Program is right for you, try one of the Honors courses.
3. To get an idea of the types of Honors Thesis that have been done, visit the online thesis archive[79] or the collection of printed theses in the Periodicals Reading Room on the second level of the Harold B. Lee Library.

---

[79] http://honors.byu.edu/content/thesis-archive

CHAPTER FIVE

Writing for Success

Unless you are preternaturally gifted, it's likely that writing isn't a breeze for you. Such is probably the case for nearly everyone, present company included. And yet, writing well is doubtless one of the most important skills you can have both as a student and later in your professional career.

Fortunately, writing well is a skill you can develop. As with other skills, becoming a better writer won't happen overnight, but through a diligent application of the principles outlined in this chapter, you will see a noticeable improvement semester by semester, year by year.

We're going to cover topics such as reading to become a better writer, setting a writing schedule, who should look over your writing, and resources available to you at BYU to make an often onerous task more enjoyable, productive, and rewarding.

Reading to Improve Your Writing

Not surprisingly, those who read regularly are generally better writers than those who don't. And the best writers read omnivorously; that is, they read across genres and even outside their discipline. Your course load will usually dictate the bulk of what you read in any given semester, but you can always round it out with enriching supplementary materials and some books just for fun.

Whatever you read, read the kind of writers you want—or need—to emulate to be successful. For example, if you have a scientific journal article due for one of your classes, take time to dive into articles similar to the one you're writing to get a feel for how scientists express themselves.[80] The same applies to every academic discipline.

Reading Strategies
Your college years can seem like four (or more) years of virtually nonstop reading and writing. As a BYU student, you will be splitting your time between classes, church service, social life, and possibly work, among other things. You will need some strategies to get through all the reading that you both need and want to do. Below we will discuss e-reading and audiobooks, our two favorite means to sneak in extra and varied reading.

E-reading
Whatever device you have, it likely has enough memory to put hundreds if not thousands of books on it.[81] Most e-devices will have access to paid ebook stores. With many interesting titles on sale for less than $5, it won't take

---

[80] Be careful here, though: Scientific brilliance doesn't always translate into brilliant science writing. Science writing can be quite terrible, in fact, for the simple reason that scientists often try too hard to impress themselves, fellow scientists, the lay public, or perhaps all three through the use—and abuse—of jargon. For this reason, we highly recommend two works by Robert A. Day and coauthors: *Scientific English: A Guide for Scientists and Other Professionals, 3rd edition*, by Day and Nancy Sakaduski, and *How to Write and Publish a Scientific Paper*, by Day and Barbara Gastel.

[81] Especially when you consider that most devices can pair with computers and often come with some free cloud memory, so you'll never have to keep literally your entire ebook library on your device.

much to build a decent library. In addition, there are a lot of books that you can get for free because they have entered the public domain.[82] Have a bunch of classic literature that you need to read for your British and American literature classes? Great! Put them on your device and cart them with you wherever you go. Want free access to more current books and magazines? The BYU library and many public libraries let you check them out for free through apps like Overdrive (see below), so sign up in Provo or at your home library and get that benefit going.

Tired of Reading but Still Need to Read?

We get it. You're reading so much that your eyes feel like falling out of their sockets. Plus, you're developing saddle sores from sitting so much, and your muscles are wasting away from disuse.

But there's more to read! What are you going to do?

You can't literally[83] be reading all the time and let the rest of your life go by the wayside. You're going to need to multitask, whether it's getting a workout in, cleaning up your apartment, or commuting to campus or to an off-campus job. Maybe you're walking to class or taking a hike or traveling on a weekend. Whatever the case may be, you can greatly benefit by tapping into the power of audiobooks.

---

[82] Kindle, iBooks, and Nook libraries, just to name a few, usually have many public domain books for free. If not, then check out Project Gutenberg where you will find many titles in a variety of formats. "Project Gutenberg." *Project Gutenberg*. Web. 28 February 2018. <http://www.gutenberg.org/>.

[83] And if you are one of those people who use *literally* to mean *not literally*, please pause your reading of this book and go rewatch the Studio C Captain Literally videos on YouTube. Then continue reading this book. You literally need it.

There are at least two great audiobook apps available, one paid and the other free, provided you have access to a subscribing library like the Harold B. Lee Library on campus. Audible is essentially a paid subscription. Once you buy a book, it's yours forever.[84] Overdrive allows you to download and read ebooks or listen to audiobooks for free. The drawback is that you don't own the books because you digitally check them out from the library and eventually they must be "returned."

Of course, there is a time and a place for slow, close reading, but sometimes you just need to get the main ideas down. Fortunately, it usually doesn't take much time before you go from listening at regular speed to listening at 1.5x speed or greater with excellent comprehension (just ask anyone who has watched the accounting videos starring Professor Norm Nemrow).[85] Listening to audiobooks will let you live a normal, free-range life while allowing you to plow through a ton of text in very little time.

There are at least three ways you can incorporate audiobooks into your regular reading regimen.

First, use audiobooks to quickly get through a large number of books required for classes. A good narrator or lecturer can make any subject come alive in ways that your imagination alone might not be able to.

Second, use audiobooks to supplement the materials you're going over in many of your courses. Are you taking a course in nutrition? Why not supplement your class with an audiobook or two on nutrition and food-

---

[84] FOR-E-VER, as Michael "Squints" Palledorous would say it. If you didn't catch the reference, go watch *The Sandlot*.

[85] Plus, if you do need to repeat a section, it's easy since it's a recording.

related topics[86] or a series of lectures on the history of food?[87] Learning about American history? Why not grab an audiobook about the debate over the United States Constitution,[88] World War II,[89] or turning points in American history?[90] There are virtually[91] innumerable audiobooks that will greatly enrich your college experience in almost any subject. Just pick some and start listening.

Third, you can use audiobooks for the pure pleasure of it. College is hard and often stressful. At times, you just need to relax and get absorbed into something completely unrelated to whatever it is you're studying. That's easily taken care of through audiobooks. Might we suggest BYU

---

[86] Such as Michael Pollan's highly readable book *In Defense of Food* and *Cooked: A Natural History of Transformation*, for instance. We could name many more.

[87] *Food: A Cultural Culinary History*, by Professor Ken Albala, produced by The Great Courses. Seriously, if you've never tried one of the Great Courses lecture series, you're in for a real treat. Nate remembers seeing them advertised in the National Geographic magazines at his grandparents' home and thinking that they were a bit cheesy and weird. Then he discovered Audible, where for about 15 clams a month he can get a Great Courses lecture series, normally valued at about $200. And the series are in many cases as good as many of the lectures you're sitting through at BYU. You can't get credit for them, but they can be an excellent way to supplement your regular lectures.

[88] *The Great Debate: Advocates and Opponents of the American Constitution*, by Professor Thomas L. Pangle, produced by The Great Courses.

[89] *World War II: A Military and Social History*, by Professor Thomas Childers, produced by The Great Courses.

[90] *Turning Points in American History*, by Professor Edward T. O'Donnell, produced by The Great Courses.

[91] Note: Not *literally*. We're pretty sure the number of extant audiobooks is finite, if very large.

alumnus Brandon Sanderson's *Mistborn* trilogy as a good place to begin?

Sadly, Nate was finished with his degrees before he discovered the joys of audiobooks.[92] But Ben really benefited from including audiobooks in his regular routine and managed to finish more than 150 unique titles prior to graduating in 2016.[93]

When to Write

Writing is like a muscle: Disuse and neglect weakens it.[94] But regularly exercise that muscle, and before long, your writing will be looking pretty diesel, ready for the writer's equivalent of the Arnold Classic.[95]

As with exercise training, writing should take place, if at all possible, at predetermined regular intervals to produce the maximal effect—lean, sexy prose.

---

[92] Nate was, however, so dedicated to extracurricular reading during his undergraduate days at BYU that he was able to (not literally) waltz into the associate dean's office in his college and get her to waive one of his gen ed civilization courses—all because he went in with a big list of all the books and articles he'd read that were relevant to the course he wanted to get out of so he could graduate on time.

[93] Ben figures it was probably closer to 175, but it's hard to tell since he's just kept on listening since then and is now above 350 unique titles, not including repeat listens.

[94] Though this is a natural metaphor for us to make since Nate was a student of the exercise sciences and Ben has been a personal trainer for years, here we are paraphrasing something that President Gordon B. Hinckley used to say regarding faith. See Hinckley, Gordon B. "Latter-day Counsel: Excerpts from Recent Addresses of President Gordon B. Hinckley." *Ensign Mar. 1999 - Ensign.* Web. 28 February 2018. <https://www.lds.org/ensign/1999/03/latter-day-counsel-excerpts-from-recent-addresses-of-president-gordon-b-hinckley?lang=eng>.

[95] In case you didn't get the references, *diesel* in this context means to be muscular, and the Arnold Classic is a very important competition in the sport of bodybuilding.

In other words, write something every day, or as frequently as possible, following a deliberate schedule.

Whether blogging, journaling, or rewriting your class notes every day, it doesn't matter what you write as much as the fact that you are making daily composition a priority and a habit. Also, maintaining your daily writing habit through any holidays and summer breaks you take will prevent atrophy.

A Case in Point

While Nate was a Resident Assistant at Helaman Halls during the 2003-2004 school year, one of his residents churned out an entire novel of some 50,000+ words in only 30 days. That's an average of at least 1,667 words per day! An incredible output.

The month we're referring to is formally called National Novel Writing Month, or NaNoWriMo. It takes place every year in November when aspiring novelists hammer out their works of fiction in the insanely short span of 30 days.[96] For the fun of it.

Anyway, Nate and his other residents marveled as their compadre churned out page after page after page of prose until, finally, he had a completed novel in hand. Just like that.

The takeaway is that a busy full-time student was able to churn out a prodigious amount of writing each day precisely because he wanted to and disciplined himself to

---

[96] "National Novel Writing Month." *NaNoWriMo*. Web. 28 February 2018. <http://nanowrimo.org/>. Also, don't forget, guys, that November is also No Shave November or Movember, wherein you grow a mustache in recognition of men's health issues, which is totally Honor Code compliant.

get it done. He deliberately planned for there to be more writing in his schedule, and he didn't let anything keep him from doing it.

You don't need to actually write a novel in a month—more likely you'll be producing essays, poems, or term papers—but we hope that you can make writing a regular and planned part of your schedule so that you become a better, more prolific writer each semester.[97]

Getting a Second Opinion

It's been well established that learning is significantly improved through feedback.[98] As a writer, you want feedback from others who will be brutally honest with you. That means you don't go to people who will only say, "Great job! I love it!"

---

[97] And if you do want to try your hand at writing a novel in 30 days, get on over to www.nanowrimo.org to get the scoop, and definitely take a gander at NaNoWriMo founder Chris Baty's book *No Plot, No Problem! Revised and Expanded Edition: A Low-stress, High-velocity Guide to Writing a Novel in 30 Days*. This section on daily writing also owes a great debt to Paul J. Silvia, author of *How to Write a Lot: A Guide to Productive Academic Writing*. One point Silvia makes, that we'll discuss a little later in this chapter, is that reading and research are a part of the daily writing process; that is, writing shouldn't be narrowly defined as the act of stringing words together to form sentences and paragraphs and papers and monographs. Reading and writing work together in a seemingly synergistic symbiosis to increase both the quantity and quality of writing you produce.

[98] For starters, read Ulrich Boser's interesting *Slate* article, 'Practice Doesn't Make Perfect,' found at Boser, Ulrich. "Practice Doesn't Make Perfect. Instead, Ask for Feedback." *Slate Magazine*. 07 Mar. 2017. Web. 28 February 2018. <http://www.slate.com/articles/health_and_science/science/2017/03/practice_doesn_t_make_perfect_feedback_does.html>. Beyond this, we'll point you in the direction of motor learning research, though we imagine that other fields have studied this phenomenon as well.

Such treacly feedback warms your heart but deceives you into thinking you're a great writer with little room for improvement. Just because you like writing, were published in your high school paper or yearbook, or got an A in high school English doesn't mean you're a great writer. At least not yet.

You're writing regularly, which is a start, but how do you get the kind of feedback that will help you be a better writer? We can think of at least four ways.

First: Compare Your Writing to Better Writing
Remember all that reading you're doing?

As long as the bulk of your reading isn't in the form of 140-character tweets or Facebook status updates, and instead draws from the *best books*, to coin a phrase,[99] then that constant contact with great writing should be teaching you a thing or two about constructing prose that's interesting, inspiring, and intelligent. (And occasionally alliterative!)

Your mind can't help but pick up on the differences between your own writing and that of established authors. Why not try and deliberately imitate some of your favorites? At first, your attempts will be a bit awkward and clumsy, like Nate as a 14-year-old at his first youth dance. In time, and after much persistence, you will not merely imitate your favorite authors; rather, you will repurpose their writing styles and form a new synthesis as your own maturing style and unique voice emerge.

One way to directly leverage your reading into improved writing is through copywork, an idea we first learned about from BYU alumna Kate McKay and her hus-

---

[99] Just kidding. We grabbed that from D&C 88:118.

band Brett's blog *The Art of Manliness*.[100] According to the McKays, copywork—the process of transcribing the written work of another writer in an effort to learn his or her craft— used to be an important component of education. It allowed students to pick up on the rhythms and cadences of great writing, while learning grammar, spelling, logic, and rhetoric as if by osmosis. It probably sounds either stupid or too good to be true, but copywork is a tried and tested method for improving your "writing chops."

Second: Find a Guide

It's a sad truth that a rigorous education in the fundamentals of English grammar, logic, and rhetoric has largely gone by the wayside in America's public education systems. Token attention is perhaps given to the parts of speech and some rhetorical devices, but it's not nearly as exacting as language and composition instruction used to be. Either that or many students don't care enough to pay attention if these things are still being taught. Sadly, when high school students arrive at their university classes, they are under prepared to handle the essay composition that is a major part of almost every class.

Nate has nearly a decade of teaching experience at two large universities. He saw many students struggle writing without straying from the topic at hand, adding unrelated extraneous information, or jumping from one argument to another. It was very clear to him that his students needed additional writing help.

If you see yourself in the foregoing description, then get yourself an English grammar guide, a manual of style,

---

[100] McKay, Brett, and Kate McKay. "Want to Become a Better Writer? Copy the Work of Others!" Blog post. *The Art of Manliness*. Web. 17 April 2018. <http://www.artofmanliness.com/2014/03/26/want-to-become-a-better-writer-copy-the-work-of-others/>.

or anything that will teach you the difference between good and bad writing, and then apply yourself to mastering the principles it outlines.[101] Learning to write well is important enough that you could profitably read or reread such works at least once a school year, if not more frequently.

To see if you're making progress, we recommend that you read something you wrote in high school or one of the earliest papers of your college career and note how far you've come in your development as a writer. Don't be surprised or too chagrined when you come across some tired cliché or hackneyed expression that you thought was special sauce and would get you noticed. If you feel embarrassed that you ever thought such things constituted good writing, then you'll know that you are making progress in your writing skills development.

Third: Get Thee to the Writing Center!

The Writing Centers are magical places staffed by skilled writing tutors who are eager to teach you to be a better writer. They can assist you in the very earliest stages of planning, researching for, and outlining your paper all the way through the final formatting to make sure you don't get docked points for not properly using MLA formatting.[102] (see chapter 15: On-Campus Resources - Writing Tutors).

---

[101] If you need a suggestion, we have found the following to be very helpful: *They Say, I Say: The Moves that Matter in Academic Writing*, by Gerald Graff and Cathy Birkenstein; *The Elements of Style*, by William Strunk, Jr., and E. B. White; *Scientific English: A Guide for Scientists and Other Professionals*, by Robert A. Day and Nancy Sakaduski ; *Eats, Shoots, and Leaves: The Zero Tolerance Approach to Punctuation*, by Lynne Truss; *Death Sentences: How Cliches, Weasel Words, and Management-Speak Are Strangling Public Language*, by Don Watson; and *Sin and Syntax: How to Craft Wicked Good Prose*, by Constance Hale. There are many others.

[102] "Welcome." *Writing Center*. Web. 28 February 2018. <http://writingcenter.byu.edu/>.

In a similar vein, having a professor or a TA look over your papers and provide constructive feedback will not only improve your writing and your grade but could also foster a mentoring relationship that you might not otherwise have. Your professor or TA is best suited to giving feedback regarding the accuracy of your paper's specific content, something the writing tutors will not do.

Whether you go to the Writing Center or have a professor or TA look over your paper, we don't recommend doing either at the last minute. It won't end up being very helpful and it may irritate those you hoped to get help from.

Fourth: Start a Reading and Writing Club

Perhaps most enjoyable of all, form yourself into a group with friends and start your own weekly reading and writing club, something along the lines of the Inklings, the literary group whose illustrious members included the likes of J.R.R. Tolkien and C.S. Lewis.[103]

Get your group together on a regular basis and require members to read some or all of the writing they are working on. Then discuss, debate, criticize, and critique the heck out of it until you force one another to not only write better but to become better thinkers to boot.

Don't make your group an echo chamber where only nice, and therefore unhelpful, things are said. Be honest with each other because you genuinely care about each other's success.

If you can't get in the same room, which is always the most preferred option, then join together in an online video conference. Such a group can also serve as a book

---

[103] For more information visit "Inklings." *Inklings - Tolkien Gateway.* Web. 28 February 2018. <http://tolkiengateway.net/wiki/Inklings>.

club of sorts where you share what you are reading and teach each other what's what and who's who. To put the importance of such a group into perspective, if there hadn't been an Inklings, there very well might never have been a *Lord of the Rings*. What great works or celebrated friendships are destined to come out of your Inklings 2.0?[104]

Revising and Editing: The Secret Sauce

No one writes a masterpiece in a single go. Instead, we write drafts—usually terrible ones—and then set about the often painful process of revising and editing.

Your first draft is often simply an exercise in getting something—anything—onto paper. Of course, you're likely working from an outline and the research notes you've taken, but outline and notes aside, first drafts are basically idea dumps onto the page.

Then, in subsequent drafts, you carefully sift the wheat from the chaff, turning a mess into a masterpiece. The key to success in this phase of the writing process is to allow yourself the time to do it. Pulling all-nighters isn't going to cut it. But if you will implement the ideas we've outlined in this chapter, you shouldn't have much trouble in the writing process.

Proofread!

We cannot stress enough the importance of reading over your papers before you turn them in so that your pro-

---

[104] Brandon Sanderson, BYU alumnus and uber-famous fantasy author, attributes his success, in part, to a writing group he belonged to while at BYU. See Sanderson, Brandon. "EUOLogy: My History as a Writer." Blog post. Web. 28 February 2018. <https://brandonsanderson.com/euology-my-history-as-a-writer/>. For more information on Brandon Sanderson's emergence as a writer, see "Writing of Epic Proportions." *BYU Magazine*. Web. 28 February 2018. <https://magazine.byu.edu/article/writing-of-epic-proportions/>.

fessors aren't laughing at you for writing *healthy snakes* when you really meant *healthy snacks*.[105] Spelling and grammar checkers cannot possibly catch everything and are not an adequate substitute for human intelligence, as is illustrated in the following poem:

I have a spelling checker,
It came with my PC.
It plane lee marks four my revue
Miss steaks aye can knot sea.

Eye ran this poem threw it,
Your sure reel glad two no.
Its vary polished in it's weigh.
My checker tolled me sew.[106]

If you find yourself with nothing to do on the weekend—and believe us, it happens even at BYU—pick up a copy of Richard Lederer's *Anguished English*[107] or any of its sequels and laugh your weekend woes away reading hilari-

---

[105] This gem of an example appeared in one of Nate's student's papers. Nate's family has used *healthy snakes* ever since to refer to snacks of any kind, healthful or otherwise. Of course, in making such a beef about proofreading for errors, we are very likely to run afoul of Muphry's Law, which states that those who fuss over errors in spelling, grammar, punctuation, and the like are at grave risk of committing such an error of their own in the very act said fussing. It's deliciously ironic. See "Muphry's Law." *Wikipedia*. Wikimedia Foundation, 12 July 2017. Web. 28 February 2018. <https://en.wikipedia.org/wiki/Muphry%27s_law>.

[106] *Candidate for a Pullet Surprise*, by Mark Eckman and Jerrold H. Zar, as quoted in Nordquist, Richard. The Spell Checker Poem. The full poem, of which we've quoted only the first two stanzas, is worth a look. Nordquist, Richard. "Read the Funny and Cautionary Spell-Checker Poem." *ThoughtCo*. Web. 28 February 2018. <https://www.thoughtco.com/spell-checker-poem-by-mark-eckman-1692348>.

[107] *Anguished English: An Anthology of Accidental Assaults on Our Language*, by Richard Lederer.

ous writing mistakes from students, who could have avoided them with a little more editing. (Seeing such mistakes is also a great way to learn how to avoid them yourself!)

Can't I Skip Freshman Composition?

Even if you aced the AP English tests, take a freshman English composition class. College is a whole new ball game, and it requires a significant improvement above high school writing to be successful. It can feel like more of a quantum leap than a natural progression from the end of your senior year of high school.

If you did well enough on the AP exams, then it would be a good idea to take an advanced freshman composition course rather than skipping it just because the AP credits allow you to. Taking a challenging freshman writing class to push your limits as a writer from the very start of your college career will develop your writing skills right out of the chute.[108] It's best not to put off writing classes, because you want to maximize the benefits of taking them as early as possible!

In Conclusion

In making a case for deliberately and consciously improving your writing, we aren't saying that at any point in your academic or professional career you will be publishing the kind of prose or poetry that wins awards (unless, of course, that is exactly what your academic and professional careers require—we're looking at you, English majors!).

Instead, we are saying that your ability to deliver writing that's clear concise, intelligent, and intelligible will

---

[108] Initially Ben was apathetic towards his freshman writing class but it ended up being one of the best classes he took at BYU. Rebecca Clarke worked hard to make Writing 150 engaging, enjoyable and valuable for her students. Not only is Mrs. Clarke one of the best teachers at BYU (just check her perfect "rate my professor" rating at http://www.ratemyprofessors.com/ShowRatings.jsp?tid=24231), but without exception, students who take her class will become better writers.

set you apart from your peers both at school and later at work. Follow the suggestions we've outlined in this chapter, and your writing experiences will be much more productive and enjoyable.

Write on!

Call to Action

1. Think of one or more of your favorite authors. What is it about their writing that you enjoy so much? Do you enjoy their writing because of how they use the language? If they write fiction, is it the way they use imagery to describe a scene, or are they particularly good at writing compelling characters? If they write nonfiction, what about their treatment of their subject(s) is most compelling to you? Write down your thoughts and share them with a friend. (Congratulations! You have just formed a reading and writing group.)

2. Find a (preferably nonfiction) book whose subject matter corresponds to one of the courses you're taking right now. Buy it or check it out and read or listen to it before your semester or term is through. Share with a friend the things you are learning and how you have enriched your class through the book you chose.

3. Take a few moments to look at your weekly schedule. Set aside some time every day specifically for reading and writing. Keep track of your progress using page counts, word counts, or some other way. Share what you have planned to do with a friend and ask him or her to hold you accountable. Then, return the favor.

CHAPTER SIX

Speaking in Tongues

Back in 2002 when Salt Lake City hosted the Winter Olympics, a Japanese television crew came to the BYU campus to record a report about the school being something of a foreign language mecca. At the last minute, the Japanese-speaking student they were hoping to interview couldn't go through with it, which threatened to ruin the whole experience. A University Communications employee stopped the first student who walked by and asked if he could speak Japanese. And—surprise!—he could, because he had recently served a mission to Japan.[109] What are the odds? Apparently at BYU they're pretty darn good.

Did you know that nearly three fourths of all BYU students speak a second language?[110] And fully one-quarter

---

[109] Sarah Jane Weaver Church News Staff Writer. "BYU's Multilingual Campus." *LDS Church News - Authorized News Web Site of The Church of Jesus Christ of Latter-day Saints.* Web. 1 March 2018. <https://www.ldschurchnewsarchive.com/articles/41254/BYUs-multilingual-campus.html>.

[110] "Bilingual BYU." *BYU Humanities.* Web. 28 February 2018. <http://humanities.byu.edu/bilingual-byu/>.

of the student body is taking a foreign language class at any given time. The national average is 8 percent.[111]

BYU is nationally recognized as being a leader in language instruction, number of language courses offered, number of students taking language courses, number of students taking advanced language courses, and more.

In addition to offering language majors and minors, BYU often has classes for less commonly spoken languages, mostly dependent on demand and an available instructor. In all, BYU has the ability to deliver courses in some 80 languages![112]

Let's get down to some nuts and bolts on how you can make the most of your foreign language experience at BYU.

Exams and Certifications
If you speak a foreign language that isn't your native language, then you can earn a bunch of BYU credits just by doing well on a big exam in lieu of taking the 100- and 200-level courses.

Challenge Exams
The first way to do this is to take a 3-credit hour, 300-level language and culture course for your target language. (Be aware that not all languages have such a course. More on that later.)

---

[111] The 25% and 8% statistics are from "Speaking in Tongues." *BYU Magazine*. Web. 28 February 2018. <https://magazine.byu.edu/article/speaking-in-tongues/>.

[112] "Center for Language Studies." *Languages Offered at BYU: All | Center for Language Studies*. Web. 28 February 2018. <https://cls.byu.edu/languages>.

Then, you sign up for the corresponding Challenge Exam, which will test your ability in listening, reading, speaking, and writing in your target language.[113]

Challenge exams have the potential to add 16 graded credit hours to your transcript! What's that? Need to boost your GPA a little? This is one quick, easy, and fun way to do it that immediately pays you for all the hard work you put in learning how to conjugate verbs in the pluperfect tense.[114]

To put the potential importance of the Challenge Exam into perspective, remember from chapter 2 that after he returned from his mission to Tokyo, Ben used the Challenge Exam to test out of 16 Japanese credits. The credits he earned from the exam combined with what he earned over a summer term put Ben at enough credits to apply to BYU as a transfer student, and he was accepted.

That's just one example. Undoubtedly, there are other ways students benefit from taking the Challenge Exams for their languages.

FLATS Exams

The second way to earn credit by examination is to take one of the exams offered through the Foreign Language Achievement Testing Service (FLATS).[115]

---

[113] "Challenge & Exemption Exams." *BYU Registrar's Office*. Web. 28 February 2018. <https://registrar.byu.edu/challenge-exemption-exams>.

[114] Don't fret. We fully realize that there are languages that don't use verb conjugation—or much inflection at all, for that matter—to indicate tense or case or what-you-will. Nate's mission language of Samoan is just such a language.

[115] Humanities, Office Of Digital. *Foreign Language Achievement Testing Service*. Web. 28 February 2018. <http://flats.byu.edu/flatsinfo.php>.

FLATS exams cover 101 through 201 language courses and give you 12 pass/fail credit hours that do not affect your GPA and cannot ever be converted to graded credit. Some languages that do not have Challenge Exams will often have a FLATS exam.

When Nate returned to school after his mission to the Samoan islands, he discovered that BYU only offered a Samoan FLATS exam. He took what he could get, but he went on to take Samoan 202 as a graded class to complete the 16 credits. Then, he was able to drum up enough support among the small Samoan-speaking student population, and with their instructor's help, they created the first ever 300-level Samoan culture class geared toward native Samoans, returned missionaries, and advanced students. It was a ton of fun, and the course has continued (off and on) since its creation in 2005. He's even heard rumors of a Samoan Challenge Exam being created.

If you find that your language is in a similar situation, we highly recommend you challenging the status quo and growing its program.

Language Certifications

If you're one of the lucky ones to have developed a proficiency in any one or more of BYU's 15 most commonly taught foreign languages,[116] then you can distinguish yourself by earning a Language Certificate.

To earn a Language Certificate, you must take a minimum of three courses, one each in the following cate-

---

[116] The 15 languages are Arabic, Chinese, Danish, Finnish, French, German, Italian, Japanese, Korean, Norwegian, Portuguese, Russian, Spanish, Swedish, and Tagalog. "Language Certificate Program Center For Language Studies." *Language Certificate Program*. Web. 28 February 2018. <https://languagecertificate.byu.edu/>.

gories: Language, Civilization, and Literature.[117] Then, you take two exams: An Oral Proficiency Interview and a Writing Proficiency Test.

About a month after you take your exams, you'll find out whether you qualify for a Language Certificate. If you do qualify, then your transcript will be annotated to show that you earned the certificate, and you will receive a printed certificate to frame and proudly display next to your diploma once you've earned that too.

BYU has financial resources available to its students to help defray the costs of the different language certification exams. Many foreign language departments will subsidize the cost of these tests and certifications for students within the department. Check it out!

Foreign Language Housing

If you want to extend your mission language experience or just take your language skills to the next level, you can always apply to live at the Foreign Language Student Residence (FLSR, pronounced *flisser*).[118] Nestled in between the Provo Temple and the MTC, the FLSR requires students to speak their target language 100% of the time they spend in their apartment. Each apartment has a native speaker living there and a lot of books and movies in the

---

[117] "Language Certificate Program Center For Language Studies." *Language Certificate Program*. Web. 28 February 2018. <https://languagecertificate.byu.edu/course-options>.

[118] By mission language, we mean ASL, Chinese, French, German, Italian, Japanese, Korean, Portuguese, Russian, or Spanish. The languages offered at the Foreign Language Student Residence (FLSR) are "contingent on student demand," according to the housing website. Accommodations, BYU Campus. "Foreign Language Student Residence." *BYU On-Campus Housing*. Web. 28 February 2018. <http://www.byu.edu/oncampushousing/flsr.shtml>.

target language, so there really is no way you won't improve on your language.

Nate had a friend who spoke Spanish from his time as a missionary in Ecuador and then went on to be a Resident Assistant at FLSR. He was a pretty ambitious guy and wanted to learn Portuguese and French, and FLSR was his ticket to obtaining a proficiency in both. Being home for dinner each weekday evening is a strict requirement, however, so make sure that you understand the time requirement involved with living at the FLSR.

Interpretation at the MTC

There's hardly anything more invigorating and simultaneously exhausting than serving as an interpreter. The Missionary Training Center is often in need of interpretation volunteers to ensure that its devotionals, firesides, and other meetings are understood by non-English-speaking elders and sisters. Much of the vocabulary used in the meetings will be familiar to any returned missionary as will the meeting format since he or she will have experienced them while in the MTC for his or her own mission.

Interpreting is a great way to keep up one's mission language while giving service at the same time, a requirement in some service-learning based courses. But it's not a cakewalk; sometimes, the speakers don't seem aware that there are interpreters trying to render their messages into another language as fast as the speakers speak.

Nate vividly remembers nearly tearing his hair out at one devotional when the speaker, a general authority, started in on a complex metaphor that drew both from baseball and golf, two sports that many native Samoans have little to no experience with, and Nate had to innovate the vocabulary on the spot. Nevertheless, all ended well, and the overall message was conveyed sufficiently to ensure understanding. (He hopes.)

TRC Volunteering at the MTC

In addition to volunteering as an interpreter at the MTC, you can always go to the Teaching Resource Center (TRC) to let the missionaries teach you in their target languages. You will bless them in multiple ways by doing so, including giving them the assurance that it is possible to learn the language. After all, you did! It's just the sort of encouragement missionaries need when they are feeling the weight of learning their mission language adequately to fulfill the prophecy that everyone will have the opportunity to hear the gospel in their own language.[119]

Teaching at the MTC

Last in our series of MTC-based opportunities is the chance to teach your language there. The MTC pays its teachers well, and teaching there is a great way to essentially continue your missionary service through the language acquisition of your students.

Some have said that it takes about 10,000 hours to become an expert at something (though there is much debate that the case has been overstated).[120] A mission with a foreign language component has the potential to give elders up to 11,680 waking hours of language exposure and sisters 8,760 hours.[121] Elders and sisters who are immersed in new

---

[119] See Doctrine and Covenants 90:11.

[120] As far as we know, the 10,000-hour rule was popularized in Malcolm Gladwell's *Outliers*. He has been criticized for overstating the case for 10,000 hours being sufficient for becoming an expert, but there is still a kernel of truth to it for use as a simple shorthand for *lots of time = significant skill development*. Two other books that have made important contributions to this discussion include *The Sports Gene* by David Epstein, and *Faster, Higher, Stronger* by Mark McClusky.

[121] Here's how we did the math. For elders, we said they'd get 16 waking hours/day x 365 days/year x 2 years = 11,680 hours. For sisters, we said they'd get 16 waking hours/day x 365 days/year x 1.5 years = 8,760. We understand that there are leap days unaccounted for here, or extensions

languages have an embarrassment of riches[122] when it comes to language learning opportunities.

To be brutally honest, though they may have reached the coveted 10,000 hours, many returned missionaries have an over-inflated opinion of their mission language skills. For example, in an interview with the *Deseret News*, BYU professor and then dean of the College of Humanities, Van C. Gessel said, "Missionaries come home claiming fluency. But it's a fluency on a very limited range of topics, like religion and 'Where's the bathroom?'"[123]

We have heard returned missionaries claim they can "speak like the natives." In our experience, when native speakers complement non-native missionaries' language skills, what they are actually communicating is that they appreciate them trying hard to learn their language but that they are still butchering it pretty badly.

Teaching language fundamentals at the MTC to new missionaries with no real language experience will do wonders for your own language ability, both in speaking and comprehending the grammar mechanics that you may have missed the first time around.

---

to missions, or missions cut short, or language reassignments, or any number of possible changes to these basic formulas.

[122] For those unfamiliar with the phrase, *embarrassment of riches* means *more than you could possibly make use of*, or, if you prefer a single word, *plethora*, *myriad*, *beaucoup*, and so forth.

[123] As quoted in Walch, Tad. "BYU Is Major U.S. Center for Language Study." *DeseretNews.com*. Deseret News, 24 Apr. 2005. Web. 28 February 2018. <http://www.deseretnews.com/article/600128849/BYU-is-major-US-center-for-language-study.html?pg=all>.

International Cinema and Media Center

The International Cinema[124] isn't going to show a film in each of the world's languages, much less do so in a single semester or school year. But if you speak one or more of the more commonly taught languages like Spanish, French, or German, chances are that there will be at least one film screened in your language of interest.

The Media Center is also a great place to look for foreign language films that you can check out or watch in one of the media viewing rooms on a big-screen TV.[125]

Call to Action

1. If you are functionally fluent in a foreign language, check to see if there is a Challenge Exam, FLATS Exam, or Language Certificate for that language. Then, make a plan for taking the available exam, earning the certificate or both. Find a friend to accept the same challenge and hold each other accountable.

2. Contact the MTC about opportunities to volunteer either as an interpreter or at the Teaching Resource Center. Then, make a plan to regularly volunteer to use your language at the MTC and help the missionaries prepare to serve.

3. If you speak a second language, find out what it takes to earn a minor in it and how to fit the language minor into your overall academic program.

---

[124] "BYU International Cinema." *BYU International Cinema*. Web. 28 February 2018. <http://ic.byu.edu/>.

[125] "BYU Harold B. Lee Library." *Media Center | HBLL*. Web. 28 February 2018. <https://sites.lib.byu.edu/mediacenter/>.

CHAPTER SEVEN

Make the World Your Campus

Have you ever wanted to experience the thrill of living in a foreign country? If experiencing a new culture or improving your foreign language skills is high on your priority list, then one of BYU's international study programs will be perfect for you. Each year, over 1,500 BYU students participate in more than 100 different international study programs in over 50 countries.[126] Participating in an international study program is the highlight of many students' BYU experience.

Mark Salisbury told NPR's Tom Gjelten regarding international study programs, "Many times it reshapes the way they [i.e. students] think about their own career plan, and they take a more reflective turn on the role that they're going to play in the world as it relates to their career plans. And oftentimes, you talk to people who studied abroad 50

[126] "International Study Programs." *Kennedy Center*. Web. 28 February 2018. <https://kennedy.BYU.edu/isp/>.

years ago, and they will tell you that that was the most powerful experience that they had."[127]

Participating in an international study program will help shape the way you understand and perceive the greater world around you. Despite what you may have heard, the world extends beyond "Happy Valley" Utah, and you will greatly benefit from experiencing as much of that outside world, its people, and cultures as possible.

Salisbury makes note of this again, stating, "Many times it really opens their eyes to a [new] way of thinking about the world that we live in and how their actions and their interactions with people from other cultures really have an effect on the world that we live in."

BYU currently offers four different types of international study programs as listed on the Kennedy Center's webpage. For a full listing of the international study programs available, visit the Kennedy Center's webpage.[128]

Study Abroad
Study abroad groups are accompanied by a BYU professor who acts as a professor and tour guide as students visit important historical and cultural locations. These programs are usually intended to support and supplement what students are learning in the classroom.

International Internships
International internships are work-focused experiences in a foreign country. Students are able to gain real-world work experience and training in their field of interest

---

[127] Staff, NPR. "Studying Abroad: Is It Really Worth It?" *NPR*. NPR, 09 Aug. 2012. Web. 28 February 2018.
<http://www.npr.org/2012/08/09/158501278/weighing-the-benefits-of-studying-abroad>.

[128] http://kennedy.BYU.edu/isp/find-your-program/

while living and working in a foreign country. These experiences are especially beneficial to students who are interested in pursuing careers in foreign countries after graduation. International interns keep in touch with a BYU faculty mentor who helps them along the way.

If we didn't have you convinced at the word *international*, let us sweeten the deal: BYU even offers a Chocolate Internship that places interns in Germany, Belgium, or the Netherlands with the Halloren chocolate company. In addition to assisting with graphic design or inventory, interns can expect to aid with product development and give feedback on samples! Delicious!

Direct Enrollment

Direct enrollment differs from a study abroad program in a few ways. First, students do not travel with BYU faculty or other BYU students like they would in a study abroad program but are instead enrolled for one or more semesters at a university campus in another country. Second, students are completely immersed in the language and culture of their host country as they attend classes and interact with natives daily. Credits accrued transfer back to BYU at the conclusion of the direct enrollment program.

Field School

Field School is a program where students with BYU faculty mentors engage in research and field study in a foreign country. In addition to being exposed to field research in exotic locations, students also benefit from exposure to their host country's language and culture.

The Price Is Right

Fortunately, most BYU-sponsored international study programs are roughly the same price as a normal semester's tuition, so they aren't prohibitively expensive. To make international study programs accessible, BYU has done a great job of putting together scholarships and financial aid packages to help offset the cost for qualifying students, which means you should apply for as many as you can.

Many off-campus scholarships, federal financial aid such as Pell Grants, and student loans can also be used to help fund your international study experience[129] (see chapter 2: Paying for School). For a list of external scholarships, visit the Kennedy Center ISP scholarship webpage for even more ways to help fund your international study program.[130] Also, check with your college's advisement center, which may have scholarships available to help you pay for your overseas adventures.

Call to Action

If participating in one BYU's many international study programs is of interest to you, do the following:

1. Visit the Kennedy Center's webpage[131] and start looking at all the different locations and types of international study programs available to choose from.

2. Begin to plan how you will finance your semester abroad. See chapter 2: Paying for School for ideas.

3. Don't hesitate to get in touch with the Kennedy Center if you have questions. The center will be able to

---

[129] Students who plan well and who are aggressively applying for scholarships and grants at every opportunity should be able to fund study abroad programs without going into debt. It is the belief of both authors of this book that students should avoid student loans whenever humanly possible. Carefully read Chapter 2: Paying for School to find out how you can fund your study abroad experience.

[130] "ISP Scholarships." *Kennedy Center*. Web. 28 February 2018. <http://kennedy.BYU.edu/ispscholarships/>.

[131] https://kennedy.byu.edu/isp/

help you make your dreams of studying abroad a reality!

CHAPTER EIGHT

Undergraduate Research

BYU ranks consistently ranks as an excellent research undergraduate university and places a huge emphasis on undergraduate research programs specifically designed for and tailored to undergraduate students.[132] BYU emphasizes undergraduate research because students who engage in research experiences are better equipped with the specific skill set and knowledge that will help them excel at their post-graduation endeavors. Undergraduate researchers are also setting themselves apart from their peers; they can get stronger letters of recommendation and build better resumes.

In 2013, Christopher R. Madan of the University of Alberta penned an excellent article titled *The Benefits of Undergraduate Research: The Student's Perspective,* in which he stated, "The undergraduate experience is greatly enriched by obtaining research experience early and often. Recently this has been demonstrated empirically and discussed at length in a variety of disciplines, including but not

---

[132] More specifically, BYU ranks #58 according to "Brigham Young University." *Forbes*. Forbes Magazine, Web. 28 February 2018. <http://www.forbes.com/colleges/brigham-young-university/>.

limited to engineering, medicine, biology, physiology, neuroscience, psychology, as well as in multidisciplinary discussions in prestigious journals."[133]

That is a lot of evidence supporting the value of getting involved in undergraduate research as early as possible, so consider how you want to get involved as you read through this chapter.

What Is Undergraduate Research?

For some young students, the word "research" may conjure up images of nerdy STEM (science, technology, engineering and math) majors in lab coats conducting Frankensteinian experiments on cute lab animals. Or, perhaps, it's Hermione types endlessly pouring over dusty tomes while secluded in the shadowy nooks of the library.

Either way, many students have had negative experiences with research assignments during high school because they were assigned boring and unfulfilling research topics or because they were simply never taught how to design and carry out good research projects. Unstructured and uninteresting research projects will always feel boring and are usually a waste of time.

Fortunately, at BYU the undergraduate research programs are designed to provide you the opportunity to work alongside and be personally mentored by a highly competent and experienced professor or faculty member doing exciting and valuable research. Oftentimes, professors will have a whole team of postdocs, graduate students, and un-

---

[133] See "The Pennsylvania State University Division of Undergraduate Studies." *The Mentor*. Web. 28 February 2018<https://dus.psu.edu/mentor/2013/05/undergraduate-research-students-perspective/>. This is a really good article, but we also felt that the research that Madan cites in the quotation is well worth the effort to find and read.

dergraduate students all working together and collaborating with each other.

You will find hundreds of professors across all 10 colleges and academic disciplines working with and mentoring students just like you. Together, these professor-student teams are studying a specific topic within their field and making real contributions that help further the understanding of their discipline. Sometimes, this collaboration results in both the professor and student being awarded grants and, ideally, publications in scholarly journals.

We want to stress the fact to you that regardless of your intended major, minor, interests, hobbies, future career aspirations, or academic background, there is most likely a research group on campus that you would find interesting! Research is not just something done by mad scientists in secret laboratories. While more often in the spotlight, the research being done in the so-called hard sciences—a term for the natural sciences such as math, biology, chemistry, and physics—is in no way more important than the research being done in the soft sciences of psychology, sociology, political science, and so forth. At BYU, the need for research in all scholarly disciplines is recognized and fostered.

Why Undergraduate Research?

If you conducted a survey and asked a hundred of your peers why they joined a research team, you would probably get about a hundred different answers.[134] In reality, there are tons of great reasons to get involved with research. This section will introduce some of the more general benefits of doing undergraduate research, but you will inevitably discover benefits beyond those listed here.

---

[134] This is a testable hypothesis, one that you could explore for your own ORCA, capstone, or Honors Thesis research project. You're welcome!

Many students have not had significant or meaningful exposure to proper research methodologies prior to admittance into college. This lack of exposure can result in a gap in the student's academic foundation. If you feel like you fall into this category, don't worry! Joining a research team and getting early exposure to the research process will help you become expert at pursuing knowledge and finding factual, data-driven answers to your questions. Academics will cease to be a long list of facts to be memorized and tucked away for later retrieval during an exam. Instead, it will become a way to think about, question, and investigate the world around you. You will be empowered to use research methodologies to discover new truths and develop a greatly amplified ability to reason, postulate, and think for yourself.

Undergraduate research also happens to be one of the strongest things you can put on a resume when applying to grad schools or seeking post-graduation employment. When admissions board members or potential employers see that an applicant has had significant undergraduate research experience, their interest is piqued; they'll want to know more about your research and about you as a potential member of their school or company.

The reason for this is simple: Research requires a lot of work and significant amounts of diligence, integrity, and self-efficacy. These are all qualities that are highly sought after in the real world, and students who are able to develop these qualities early will be highly sought after as a result.

If you are considering setting your sights on graduate school, then undergraduate research experience is a critical activity to have listed on your resume. As a graduate student, you will spend a significant amount of time doing research. Graduate school admissions want to know that you have a rock-solid research background and that you really understand what you are signing up for at their institution. Addressing the importance of undergraduate research experience for prospective graduate students, Chris Burge, a biology professor at MIT, was quoted in Science Magazine saying, "If you're going to be doing research full-time in graduate school, why would you go through your whole undergraduate experience and never try it?"[135]

In an increasingly competitive world, more and more students are taking the initiative and spending their undergraduate years involved in as many resume-building activities as possible. Just as admission to BYU is getting increasingly competitive each year, admission into graduate programs and qualifying for good, high-paying jobs is also getting unbelievably competitive. It is no longer enough for you to simply graduate from BYU with decent grades and expect to land your dream job. Employers are increasingly looking for applicants who have work history and on-the-job experience. A significant research experience is absolutely, hands down, one of the very best ways you can gain real-world work experience, hone your competitive edge, and ensure that you stand out against your competition. While your peers are working low-paying jobs after graduation to build up work experience, the time you spent working in a research lab will provide that needed experience and help you get better jobs right out of school.

In addition to providing you with the incredibly valuable opportunity of being directly mentored by a professor, the relationships you build with your mentor and fellow team members will turn into very powerful letters of recommendation further down the road. For many of Ben's research group mates, the letters of recommendation given by the professors they collaborated with were instrumental in helping them gain admittance to medical schools, dental

---

[135] Webb, Sarah A. "The Importance of Undergraduate Research." *Science | AAAS*. 12 Jan. 2016. Web. 28 February 2018. <http://www.sciencemag.org/careers/2007/07/importance-undergraduate-research>.

schools, and graduate programs at schools like Stanford, Harvard, and Notre Dame. These professors personally knew each student from years of working together, and they wrote powerful endorsements of the students' work ethic, ability to collaborate, and overall preparedness for the graduate programs they were applying for. If you get involved in a research lab, work hard, and are teachable, you will build the relationships necessary for incredibly influential letters of recommendation when you need them.

Get Paid

In case we haven't been able to convince you to race out and join a research team yet, there is plenty of money to be had as well! To encourage students to get involved, many organizations around campus provide grants to students doing undergraduate research. For example, the Office of Research and Creative Activities (ORCA) awards $1,500 grants to students involved with one-on-one mentoring with a processor or qualified faculty member (see chapter 2: Paying for School - Other Scholarships and Grants). That's $1,500 on top of an already rewarding opportunity working one-on-one with an expert in your field! The Honors Department also has several grants and scholarships available for undergraduate researchers (see chapter 4: Honors Program).

Additionally, many professors are regularly applying for external grants and funding that provide the lab with money to purchase supplies, cover research costs, and even pay stipends to student researchers. While not every student will secure a coveted paid position on the research team, when there is extra funding available, professors will often choose to give especially hard-working students an hourly wage.

All five research teams Ben worked with had students who were receiving stipends of one kind or another. The amount of their stipends varied based upon their experience in the lab, the difficulty of the projects they were undertaking, and whether or not the research was helping to generate additional funding for the team. Some students preferred to earn credit hours for the time spent working on their research instead of an hourly wage—a great way for students to buff up their GPA (see chapter 13: Improving Your Science GPA). Several students were awarded prestigious grants to do research for companies like Chevron Corporation and Exxon. Other students helped develop products that were commercialized and sold or leased to large companies.[136]

Ben spent a summer working with the BYU Phage Hunter bee team, which has spent several years researching bacteria-killing phages that can be used to treat the incredibly dangerous American Foulbrood (AFB) bacteria.[137] These phages are a very promising solution that can prevent and even destroy AFB bacteria without harming the bees or contaminating the honey. Additionally, phage treatment is helping prevent the need for beekeepers to use costly and increasingly ineffective antibiotics. The Phage Hunters have since begun marketing its product for mass production and sale, and the team is seeking FDA approval. The Phage Hunters have an excellent webpage[138] and

---

[136] When it comes to commercializing research discoveries, BYU is no small fry. Check out: "BYU No. 4 in the Country for Taking Research Inventions to Market." *Brigham Young University*. 03 July 2017. Web. 28 February 2018. <http://news.byu.edu/news/byu-named-one-nation%E2%80%99s-best-commercializing-research-innovations>.

[137] "Related Topics." *American Foulbrood Disease : USDA ARS*. Web. 28 February 2018. <https://www.ars.usda.gov/northeast-area/beltsville-md/beltsville-agricultural-research-center/bee-research-laboratory/docs/american-foulbrood-disease/>.

[138] "Mmbio-BYU Phage Hunters." *YouTube*. YouTube, 12 June 2013. Web. 28 February 2018. <https://www.youtube.com/watch?v=Wzi-2qG-C70>.

YouTube videos[139] that really give you a sense of how fun and exciting research can be. This is just one example of undergraduate students doing groundbreaking research with significant real-world application.

Publications

The ultimate achievement of any research effort is to publish original findings in a prestigious academic journal. Often, publications will be accompanied by presentations of the research to peers, other researchers, and subject matter experts at large conventions. For professional and student researchers alike, this is equivalent to winning the Superbowl because the massive majority of research projects will never make it to publication for one reason or another.

Remember this: The impact of publications will last long after you move on to graduate school or your dream job. Michael Doyle, former president of the Council on Undergraduate Research[140] and chemistry professor at the University of Maryland, hit the nail on the head when he said that a publication—unlike a GPA, which at best only helps for a few years—"lasts a lifetime."[141]

---

[139] "Bee Killers: Using Phages Against Deadly Honeybee Diseases." *YouTube*. 27 Oct. 2014. Web. 28 February 2018. <https://youtu.be/rj9_QGBJNow>.

[140] *"CUR - The Council on Undergraduate Research." The Council on Undergraduate Research - Learning Through Research | Membership, Publications, Conferences & Events, Projects & Services, Governance, Advocacy and Resources | Council on Undergraduate Research. Web.* 28 February 2018. <*http://www.cur.org/*>.

[141] Sarah A. Webb Jul. 6, 2007 , 8:00 AM, 2016 Elisabeth PainMar. 21, 2017 Beryl Lieff Benderly Jun. 7, 2016 Elisabeth PainSep. 22, and 2017 Maggie Kuo Jun. 5. "The Importance of Undergraduate Research." *Science | AAAS.* 12 Jan. 2016. Web. 28 February 2018. <http://www.sciencemag.org/careers/2007/07/importance-undergraduate-research>.

It is still quite uncommon for an undergraduate student to gain publications as either a principal or coauthor because it does take such a considerable amount of time and work. However, if you get involved early and are persistent until the completion of the research project, you could be one of the select few who graduate from BYU as a published author!

Finding Research Opportunities

If you are ready to start getting involved with a research team, there are several excellent places to begin. The first place to start looking for research opportunities is with the professors of your favorite classes. It is very likely that many of your favorite professors are involved with ongoing research programs. At the very least, they will be able to direct you to other faculty members who are mentoring student researchers. Additionally, faculty who are not already involved with research are perfect to approach about collaborating on an ORCA grant (see chapter 2: Paying for School - Other Scholarships and Grants) or work with you as an advisor on an Honors Thesis (see chapter 4: Honors Program) or capstone project.

College advisement offices will often have a list of the ongoing research projects of all the professors in the department. If you are uncertain what type of research interests you, this can be a great way to see what research teams are already established in your department and learn about the cool things they are working on.

The Honors Department is another wonderful resource to help you find a faculty mentor who can help guide you as you design and conduct your own unique research project. Indeed, one of the core learning outcomes of the Honors Department is to help students "develop, articulate, and conduct research on the questions—great or narrow—

that interest [them] with the appropriate and accepted academic methodologies, practices, and conventions."[142]

Many major programs require a final research project, often referred to as a "capstone" project, before students are cleared for graduation. These projects will vary in scope and requirements between programs, but they are usually expected to show original, well-thought-out and conducted research and to be followed up with a paper or presentation. Many students choose to combine their capstone project with an ORCA grant project, Honors Thesis, or mentored research they are already doing.

If you are interested in international studies, the BYU Kennedy Center has research opportunities and does provide grants for a limited number of students researching international relations or related topics (see chapter 2: Paying for School).

Whether you choose to research the role of telomeres in physiological aging, how different foreign language acquisition methods affect the formation of long-term memory, or the importance of gender roles in Shakespearean literature, you will gain an increased level of expertise in your research topic. You will also benefit from mastering the specific research methods of your discipline and learning how to plan and conduct quality research. This will teach you how to think critically as you analyze the world around you—definitely a valuable skill!

Call to Action

1. Visit your departmental office and inquire about the ongoing research that professors in your department are involved with.

---

[142] "BYU Honors." *Learning Outcomes | BYU Honors*. Web. 28 February 2018. <http://honors.BYU.edu/learning-outcomes>.

2. Ask your favorite professors about the research projects they are working on. If they are not currently engaged in research, ask what research opportunities they are aware of.

3. Visit the ORCA[143] and Honors Program[144] webpages if you are interested in designing and conducting your own original research project.

---

[143] https://orca.byu.edu/orca/

[144] http://honors.byu.edu/

CHAPTER NINE

Internships

Internships are programs that pair students with companies and other organizations for a short time period during which the student will work for and be mentored by the company. Like undergraduate research, internships are an excellent way for students to gain valuable on-the-job training and real-world work experience during their undergraduate years.

Unlike most undergraduate research programs, however, internships allow students to "test drive" a company they are interested in working for before actually graduating. One of the best aspects of doing an internship is being able to find one that fits your already busy schedule. Some internships will span several months, perhaps over a summer, while others will only require a few hours a week during a normal semester.

Paid vs. Unpaid Internships

Internships come in two main flavors: Paid and unpaid. If you get a paid internship, you will become essentially a short-term employee for the company for the duration of the internship period. Students with unpaid internships will receive some training from the employer, work and collaborate on projects, and get a look behind the scenes, but they will not be expected to put in the same number of hours as a paid intern.[145]

While not a hard rule, unpaid internships tend to be with nonprofits, small businesses, and governmental organizations while paid internships are often offered by large, well-funded corporations. Corporations offering paid internships are also more likely than nonprofit organizations to recruit new hires straight from a pool of interns.

According to a 2014 report from the National Association of Colleges and Employers, there are several reasons for this:

> "First, it could be that companies with the resources to afford paid internships are also more likely to have resources to hire those interns later. Eighty percent of employers consider internships to be a recruiting tool, but larger, for-profit companies frequently are better able to afford to pay students, while smaller government offices and nonprofits may be unable to do so. The latter two types of organizations generally have less turnover and fewer resources to hire someone new as well."[146]

---

[145] While these descriptions are accurate, there will always be exceptions. *U.S. Department of Labor - Wage and Hour Division (WHD) - Fact Sheet.* Web. 28 February 2018. <https://www.dol.gov/whd/regs/compliance/whdfs71.htm>.

[146] "Why Are Paid Interns More Likely to Get Job Offers?" *Education Advisory Board.* Web. 28 February 2018. <https://www.eab.com/daily-briefing/2015/05/07/why-are-paid-interns-more-likely-to-get-job-offers>.

Each type of internship will provide different experiences and be uniquely valuable to you. Whether paid or unpaid, the time spent interning will pay dividends when you graduate and move on to postgraduate pursuits.

Internships Have Real Value

Research shows that students who engage in one or more internships during their undergraduate career will have up to a 28% better chance of receiving one or more job offers *before* graduation.[147] Each year, hiring businesses are increasing their emphasis on hiring graduates with more work experience. Matt Sigelman, CEO of a leading labor market analytics firm, emphasized, "Employers want people to come to the workplace with a set of both technical and foundational skills. The more summers you can spend accruing those skills, the more of a track record you can demonstrate to employers."[148]

Many departments at BYU also allow you to get credit for approved internships. Internship credits are helpful for students who need to maintain a certain credit threshold to maintain eligibility for academic scholarships, involvement with sports, or Pell Grants. Gaining credits for your internship experience can also be a smart way to bump up your GPA. Just remember that if you get too many credits, you will eventually run out of eligibility for Pell Grants and academic scholarships, so plan accordingly (see chapter 3: Majors, Minors, Etc. - How Declaring a Major Early Can Help Scholarship Chances). For more infor-

---

[147] "Benefits of Internships." *Benefits of Internships*. Web. 28 February 2018. <https://intern.BYU.edu/content/benefits-internships>.

[148] "Why Are Paid Interns More Likely to Get Job Offers?" *Education Advisory Board*. Web. 28 February 2018. <https://www.eab.com/daily-briefing/2015/05/07/why-are-paid-interns-more-likely-to-get-job-offers>.

mation about the exact credit limit, contact the BYU Financial Center and University Advisement Center.

Finding the Perfect Internship

The David M. Kennedy Center for International Studies has established international internship programs available for students seeking to intern with foreign companies. These programs are an excellent way for students to get work experience and training while improving their foreign language skills (see chapter 7: Make the World Your Campus – Study Abroad) and are also a great way to travel and experience foreign cultures and countries.

Both Ben and Nate had friends who spent a semester doing internships with companies in Japan. They both noted how much their understanding of Japanese culture had grown, and they noticed many interesting differences working for a Japanese company versus an American company. Their time working in Japan was very beneficial to their language skills as they were exposed to both colloquial and business-type vocabulary and grammar principles they had not been exposed to as missionaries in Japan. International internships usually involve a longer application process, but many are available at different times throughout the year.

If you prefer a domestic experience, there are internships that will take you away from Provo to other parts of the country, and others are available right on BYU campus. Nate completed a significant internship experience right on campus at Y-Be-Fit helping students and BYU staff, faculty, and administration members achieve their fitness goals (see chapter 2: Paying for School - On-Campus Employment). During his last semester at BYU, Ben interned with an exciting startup company called Emmersion Learning. He helped design online English language tutoring curriculum and aided with the creation of an online, automated English language proficiency test. He worked online around his own schedule and received a lot of great mentoring from the CEO of the company over Skype. For Ben, the ability to work remotely and at odd hours was a perfect fit whereas Nate had set hours he had to be at the Y-Be-Fit office on campus.

With the many internship opportunities available to you at BYU, you will easily be able to find the perfect internship. So get looking!

Some great places to begin your search for the perfect internship include:

- Your college's Academic Advisement Center
- Department Internship Coordinator
- BYU Internship Office
- Certain STDEV classes
- David M. Kennedy Center for International Studies
- Professors involved with research
- Job and career fairs

Be the Best Intern of the Bunch
Regardless of what kind of internship you do, there are some tips that will help you get the most out of your experience as possible. These tips are part of a longer article about internship do's and don'ts written by Dr. Randall S. Hansen, founder of Quintessential Careers and CEO of the website EmpoweringSites.com.[149] A few of the tips Dr. Hansen gives to students include:

- Obtain at least one if not multiple internships.
- Set specific goals for yourself to help you maximize what you accomplish.

---

[149] "Internship Do's and Don'ts for College Students." *Quintessential LiveCareer*. Web. 28 February 2018. <https://www.livecareer.com/quintessential/internship-dos-donts>.

- Set regular meeting times with your internship supervisor whether in person, on the phone, or over a video call.
- Make sure you leave your internship having learned new skills and with a better understanding of the field.
- After your internship has concluded, keep in touch with your old friends and acquaintances as these relationships may lead to jobs or other opportunities.
- Be sure to find a mentor at the company you intern with who will give you constructive criticism and help you grow.
- Don't expect internships to be handed to you; get out and hunt them down yourself.
- Be sure to avoid burning any bridges, even if your internship experience was unenjoyable.

Call to Action
1. Take a good look at the next few months of your schedule and consider how you add an internship into the mix.
2. Begin working your way through the bulleted list on page 99 to find an internship that interests you.

CHAPTER TEN

Mentoring

Mr. Miyagi. Yoda. Splinter. What do they have in common? They were all consummate mentors who imparted timeless lessons to their Daniel-San, their Padawan, their teenage mutant ninja turtles.

It's vitally important that you have a mentor (or mentors) while you move through your college years. It can make the difference between four years of unfocused wandering through academic no-man's land and tremendous success. Maybe that's a bit extreme, but the underlying and absolutely true principle is that good mentors can make a big difference in your years at BYU and beyond.

No doubt you have already had some great mentors. Perhaps a coach or a church leader or a parent or employer stands out in your mind. What was it that made him or her so effective as a mentor?

Characteristics of a Good Mentor

There are many desirable traits of a good mentor, so this list is by no means meant to be exhaustive:

Good mentors are full of experience, both theoretical and practical.

Good mentors know there are limits to their knowledge and experience.

Good mentors allow their protégés to experience life for themselves.

Good mentors desire their protégés' success more than they desire their protégés to follow their advice.

Good mentors are like a cafeteria chef: They present all kinds of options but let their protégés choose for themselves.

Good mentors are neither domineering nor driven by their own ego. They don't seek to mold their protégés into any specific shape but help them reach their full potential. They most certainly aren't out to create miniature versions of themselves. The advice and guidance they give is freely given with the understanding that their protégés must learn to discern which if any of their advice actually proves useful.

Since every path in life is unique, good mentors generally won't speak in absolutes but rather in terms of what might be given different scenarios. Since they cannot see the future, good mentors limit their advice to possibilities rather than inevitabilities.

Good mentors will defer to their protégés' best judgment, knowing that they must live with the outcomes of those decisions and not the mentor.

Where to Find a Mentor
There are at least four different sources for finding mentors during your college years: family, older students, professors, and employers. We'll consider each type in the following sections.

Family

Family members, including parents, aunts, uncles, grandparents, and older siblings, often fit the bill quite nicely as a mentor.

The older your family members are, the more dated their college experience will be, but the more likely they will understand how college attendance relates to the real world of working a job. Your older siblings and cousins, on the other hand, are more likely to have an up-to-date view of what college is like right now because they either are at college or recently graduated.

The primary difficulty with having family members as mentors is that it can sometimes be difficult to separate the familial relationship from the mentoring relationship.

Older Students

Older, more experienced students, whether upperclassmen or graduate students, can be great mentors since they're often just out of the trenches that you're now in. They may have had the same professors you now have and can help you navigate the ins and outs of school, social life, work, and church activity to find the right balance between them all. Their perspective can be invaluable as you make your way through your program.

Beware, however, of those students who wear rosy glasses and can find nothing wrong with their college experience, and also beware the students on the other extreme who seem to have an ax to grind with everything and everybody. Neither type will be great sources of information.

You want to find those fair-minded and levelheaded types who can speak to the strengths of your university, department, program, and professors without glossing over the areas needing improvement.

Professors

Professors can be great mentors. Getting in with a professor (or two) as your mentor is a great way to get ahead in your undergraduate career. It could be a professor you're a Teaching Assistant for, one who oversees a research project you are on, or one who is serving as your Honors Thesis advisor. You'll always want to remind yourself that you are not that professor's only student, so you can't monopolize his or her time or resources.

Employers

Another mentor possibility is your supervisor at any job you might hold during your undergraduate years. It could be a professor, which we discussed above, or it could be someone at an off-campus job that you could see yourself continuing after you graduate. You'll want to make sure an employer understands that you want help making the kinds of connections that will help you land that first big job after graduation.

What to Do with Conflicting Advice

It shouldn't surprise you if you have different mentors for different seasons of your undergraduate years. It also shouldn't surprise you if you have multiple mentors at the same time. If so, you will want to be ready for the inevitable and often stressful experience of getting conflicting guidance from two different mentors. When that happens, you can feel like you're stuck between a rock and a hard place.

Let us cut this Gordian knot for you, if you'll forgive us for mixing our metaphors.

If you get advice from one mentor that conflicts with the advice from another, you cannot be a people pleaser and try and do both. "No man can serve two masters," Jesus taught his disciples.[150]

Since you understand that a mentor isn't your master, that you aren't beholden to anything—let us repeat that: Anything at all—that your mentor shares with you, you don't have to feel trapped by conflicting advice.

A mentor is there to be your sounding board, to be an idea generator, to help you see things you haven't seen before and illuminate the possibilities that lay before you. A mature mentor-mentee relationship will always honor your final judgment and agency to choose for yourself the path you ultimately take. The moment you sniff the odor of compulsion in your relationship with your mentor, it is a sign that you need to move on before the relationship becomes truly toxic.

Having a mentor doesn't mean you do everything the mentor says; it means learning from his or her wisdom and experiences and adapting the best advice to your specific circumstances.

One Last Tip

Even if you don't consider them mentors, get to know your professors. Ask them questions. Answer their questions in class. Then, they will know who you are if you do need to ask for help.

There is no way you could possibly establish a true mentor in every one of your professors, either for reasons of differences in interest, personality, available time, or other factors. In defense of the professor, most of his or her time spent with students in true mentorship is going to be with his or her graduate students and a select few undergradu-

---

[150] Matthew 6:24.

ates who are helping with his or her research or teaching program.

However, you *should* take the time and make the effort to have quality interactions with each of your professors. Go up and introduce yourself early in the semester. Ask questions in class or go to his or her office hours if your questions need more thorough explanations or aren't necessarily on topic for that day's lesson. Answer questions in class.

The positive interactions you have with your professors may lead to opportunities for future mentoring to take place. At the very least, you'll establish yourself as a serious student who is wholeheartedly engaged in making your educational experience the best it can be.[151]

Your Turn

While it may seem obvious that you'll need mentors throughout your college years and beyond, perhaps it hasn't yet occurred to you that you'll also need to become a mentor.

What characteristics do you still need to develop to ensure you're the kind of mentor you would like to have?

Call to Action

1. Make a list of skills you'd like to develop or projects you'd like or have to do while at BYU. Next, make a list of potential mentors who can help you develop those skills or accomplish your projects. Contact at least one of the prospective mentors on your list and

---

[151] Again, Nate can attest to the tremendous impact that one engaged student can have on the dynamic of a lesson, having taught multiple sections of the same class in the same semester and feeling like one class was fantastic and another just dead for lack of student participation.

set up a brief, 15-minute visit where you'll explain what you want to accomplish and why you would like him or her to mentor you. If the answer is no, repeat the process until someone says yes.

2. Early in this chapter, we listed a number of characteristics we look for in a mentor. Create your own list of desirable mentor characteristics. Make a plan for developing those characteristics in yourself so that you can be the type of mentor you would like to have.

3. Think of someone who has mentored you in the past. List some of the characteristics that made him or her a good mentor. Now, list some ways you grew because of his or her mentoring. Write a thank-you letter and share some of the most important things you've written down.

CHAPTER ELEVEN

Networking

You have probably heard that the best way to get a job is by knowing someone who can hook you up. You have probably already been, or at least know of, someone who scored an awesome job through one of their friends or acquaintances. BYU reports that 65-70% of all jobs are found through networking while just submitting applications results in being hired only 1% of the time.[152] The fact of the matter is that if two equally qualified applicants are applying for the same job position, the one who has an established relationship with someone at the company will have a sizeable advantage over the other applicant. This is especially true if the relationship is with someone on the management team or with the person doing the hiring!

Networking, or the idea of getting to know people and making new friends and acquaintances in the hopes that it will lead to future career or business opportunities, is believed to be so important that it has become big business in and of itself. The online networking platform LinkedIn reported almost half a BILLION users during the second

---

[152] "University Career Services." *Networking | University Career Services*. Web. 28 February 2018. <https://ucs.BYU.edu/networking>.

half of 2016.[153] That is 500,000,000 people who spent a significant amount of time and effort setting up detailed profiles hoping to establish business relationships with more people.

Spontaneous Networking

There are ample opportunities to do some networking of your own at BYU. In fact, much of the best networking you can do will naturally happen as you participate in clubs, service projects, extramural sports teams, ward events, research and study groups, and internships and by just going to class and interacting with your peers. Get to know people, make friends, and keep tabs on what other people are doing, where they are working, the graduate schools they get accepted to, etc. These connections could help you get an internship, land the perfect job, or get into your dream school sometime down the road.

Additional Resources

If you are interested in doing a little extra networking, BYU has done a great job of providing some really great options to help you out. The University Career Services center has a lot of resources on its webpage to help you master LinkedIn and other social media sites. You'll also find guidelines to teach you how to create your personal marketing or "elevator pitch" and the basics of acing any networking event you attend.

BYU has several valuable programs and tools that will help you connect with alumni and other professionals to expand your network. Workshops and events focused on networking are regularly hosted by the Humanities department, the newly rolled out BYU Bridge program and the various BYU-sponsored career fairs. Another particular-

---

[153] "Number of LinkedIn Users." *Statista*. Web. 28 February 2018. <https://www.statista.com/statistics/274050/quarterly-numbers-of-linkedin-members/>.

ly notable program is the Take a Cougar to Lunch Program, which is hosted by the BYU Student Alumni Association. Interested students can sign up to be taken to lunch by an alumnus or other professional of their choice. This is a fantastic opportunity for you to meet one-on-one with someone who is successfully accomplishing what you are interested in doing yourself. You can get personalized, relevant advice and tips all while making a connection with someone in your field of interest.

If you are interested in networking, check out all the resources available to you on the University Career Services webpage as well as the Alumni Career Services page.[154] Both organizations are continually hosting events, posting helpful tips, and helping students and alumni make meaningful connections that often pay off big.

For entrepreneurial-focused networking, the entrepreneurship club at BYU has excellent volunteer mentors available to help students realize their ideas and ambitions. If that sounds like what you need, the Rollins Center for Entrepreneurship and Technology webpage[155] has all the info you need to get you paired with an entrepreneurial mentor.

Call to Action

1. Join a club and meet new people.
2. Commit details about the people you meet to memory so you have something to talk to them about during future encounters.
3. Engage in one of BYU's many networking events.

---

[154] "Professional Assistance for BYU Alumni." *Alumnicareers.byu.edu*. Web. 28 February 2018. <http://alumnicareers.byu.edu/>.

[155] http://marriottschool.byu.edu/cet/

4. Find a mentor who is established in the field you are interested in. (see chapter 10: Mentoring).

CHAPTER TWELVE

Service Opportunities

The BYU motto—posted on the front entrance for everyone to see—is "Enter to Learn, Go Forth to Serve." But if you wait until after graduation day to do any serving, you will have missed a good four or so years of soul-expanding experiences. There are countless ways to do service while pursuing your undergraduate studies. You can practically walk across campus on any given day and find some way to serve. The opportunities are that abundant.

Let's look at some of the resources there are on campus.

Where to Serve

Y-Serve is a program offered through the Center for Service and Learning, located in the WILK.[156] Y-Serve consists of 70 different programs designed to "serve individuals who have cognitive or physical disabilities, children and the elderly, at-risk children, and provide humanitarian ser-

---

[156] "Y - Serve |." *What Is Y-Serve.* Web. 28 February 2018. <https://yserve.BYU.edu/>.

vice."[157] After you've logged 10 hours of service through Y-Serve, you can get a certified service record, which can become an important part of your resume for future applications to jobs, internships, and post-baccalaureate and professional degree applications.[158] According to the Center for Service and Learning website, in 2015, BYU students logged 102,560 hours of community service, which was estimated at a value of over $2.5 million![159] That's both normal for BYU students and remarkable all the same.

The wards and stakes to which you will belong while you're at BYU will also host regular service projects. We've seen anything from blood drives to putting together hygiene kits, from indexing records for family history and genealogical work to volunteering at the Missionary Training Center, and much, much more, all designed to make the world a better place without a thought for recognition or self-aggrandizement.

Many of the on-campus clubs will also sponsor service projects as a way to give back to the community. Some clubs—such as the World Literacy Club or the Refugee Empowerment Club—exist primarily to provide service opportunities with a specific mission in mind.[160]

---

[157] "Our Mission and History." *Our Mission and History.* Web. 28 February 2018. <https://yserve.BYU.edu/content/our-mission-and-history>.

[158] "Service Leadership Record." *Service Leadership Record.* Web. 28 February 2018. <https://yserve.BYU.edu/content/service-leadership-record>.

[159] "Our Mission and History." *Our Mission and History.* Web. 28 February 2018. <https://yserve.BYU.edu/content/our-mission-and-history>.

[160] "Find Your Niche." *Find Your Niche.* Web. 28 February 2018. <https://clubs.BYU.edu/>.

Love Is All You Need

"Love," taught the Prophet Joseph Smith, "is one of the chief characteristics of Deity and ought to be manifested by those who aspire to be the sons [and daughters] of God. A man [or woman] filled with the love of God is not content with blessing his [or her] family alone, but ranges through the whole world, anxious to bless the whole human race."[161]

Sure, service is fun, and it often brings with it great social experiences. It looks good on a resume and will help you get future jobs, internships, or admittance to another degree program. But the primary reason for giving service is, and always should be, love for God and love for our brothers and sisters throughout the world.

Call to Action

1. In addition to the one-off service projects you will undoubtedly be a part of at BYU, chose an ongoing service project that you can regularly do for an entire semester, school year, or undergraduate degree. Make it something that resonates with you personally or allows you to share specific talents or skills you may have while serving.

2. Service opportunities are everywhere, and they don't have to be big or highly organized to matter. Find someone to serve today. It could be a friend, a roommate, a classmate, a professor, a complete stranger, your spouse...we think you get the point. Just get out there today and serve someone!

3. Find a service opportunity that is likely to take you out of your comfort zone. Perhaps it will be with

---

[161] "Teachings: Joseph Smith Chapter 37: Charity, the Pure Love of Christ." *Teachings: Joseph Smith*. Web. 28 February 2018. <https://www.lds.org/manual/teachings-joseph-smith/chapter-37?lang=eng>.

people who have special needs, the homeless, the elderly, prisoners, women and children at an abuse shelter, or recovering addicts. Take a friend and grow outside of yourself.

CHAPTER THIRTEEN

Improving Your Science GPA

For many students, their science GPA is a constant source of stress, anxiety, and worry—and for good reason. Many graduate schools and professional programs—including medical, pharmaceutical, physician assistant, dental, and veterinary programs—take a close look at an applicant's science GPA. Most institutions have GPA cut-offs that must be met before applicants are even considered for acceptance.

For example, a student graduating BYU with an overall GPA of 3.6, a science GPA of 2.9, lots of service hours, a great leadership experience, strong letters of recommendation, and several years of research in an on-campus biology lab would not be considered by the University of Utah School of Medicine, which has a strict science GPA cutoff of 3.0.[162]

---

[162] "Admissions Recommendations." *Admissions Recommendations - U of U School of Medicine - | University of Utah*. 09 June 2017. Web. 28 February 2018. <http://medicine.utah.edu/students/programs/md/admissions/>.

Many students struggle keeping their science GPA high while taking the difficult math and science prerequisites required by their prospective programs. It is easy for unwary students to get behind and do poorly in these classes. While there is no magic way to ace these classes, here are some proven strategies that will set you up for success.

Spread Out Difficult Prerequisite Classes

You may find it tempting to wait until your junior or senior year to start the chemistry and physics prerequisites you need to take. This can, and usually does, have disastrous results. For most students, even the freshman-level classes like Chem 105 will require so much study time that students run into serious trouble if they have also signed up for other time-intensive classes during the same semester. It's easy for students in this predicament to become incredibly stressed, perform poorly, and fall farther and farther behind. Sometimes, these students unwisely push through to the subsequent class only to find that the next class is even more difficult without a firm understanding of the basics. When this happens, the student's poor grades could get worse and easily destroy their chance of making it to the next level.

Don't fall into this trap! Start working on your difficult prerequisite classes early and spread them out. Draw out a flexible plan of each semester in advance so that you can make sure you have plenty of study time to dedicate to acing difficult classes.

Get Research Credit

For most post-undergraduate programs, the science GPA is calculated using only classes that fall into the math, chemistry, biology, and physics departments. This means that classes in the dietetics, food science and nutritional science, exercise science, and public health departments—while absolutely scientific in nature—do not contribute to your science GPA. However, any class that falls within the math, chemistry, biology, or physics department does count towards your science GPA, including any research lab credits earned in those departments.[163]

To get research credits, seek out and join a research group located within the chemistry, physics, biology, and math departments. Once you have been accepted into a lab, you will be given a code allowing you to add a specific mentored research class to your schedule in the same way you register for your other classes. The number of credits you can add will be decided between you and your professor prior to you adding the class.

For example, if you are interested in joining a biochemistry research group, you could seek out the professor in charge and then get the code to join the class Chem 497R - Mentored Learning in Biochemistry. Depending on how many hours you work in the lab each week, you and your mentor would decide on the appropriate number of credit hours. Because the credits you are receiving for your work in the biochem lab are awarded to you by the chemistry department, they will contribute to your science GPA.

In addition to helping you pump up your science GPA, accumulating research credits is also extremely beneficial in helping you learn the subject material, get strong letters of recommendation, potentially publish an article in a scientific journal, earn scholarship and grant money, and get a hands-on preview of the life of a scientist in that particular field (see chapter 8: Undergraduate Research).

---

[163] One notable exception to this is the American Association of Colleges of Osteopathic Medicine, which does not include math courses when calculating the science GPA of applicants to osteopathic medical schools. For more information, refer to *AACOMAS Course Subjects*. Web. 28 February 2018.
<http://help.unicas.com:8888/aacomasHelpPages/instructions/academic-history-2/aacomas-course-subjects/index.html>.

Use Introductory-Level Science Courses

Courses like Chem 101, Math 100 and 110, and Biology 100 are not required classes to get into medical or dental school, however taking them can help strengthen your science GPA in two big ways. First, they are a great introduction for students who have little or no experience with a given scientific discipline or who may just want a refresher on the material. These classes are typically relatively simple and slow paced, but for students who feel shaky about taking Chem 105 and 106, for example, taking Chem 101 and Math 110 would be a fantastic way to get you prepared for Chem 105 and 106.

The second way these classes can be a boost is because acing these classes will also count towards your science GPA. Some students may find that these classes are too easy and wish to jump in at the freshmen-level classes, and that is totally fine. Just do what will help you be most successful in the long run.

While your science GPA is just one part of your overall application to grad school, it is a very important part. Start now and do everything you can to have a strong science GPA. When you graduate, you will thank yourself a thousand times over.

Call to Action

1. Plan your semesters far enough in advance to ensure that you don't have to cram in too many difficult science classes into your last few semesters.
2. Don't overlook introductory-level science courses if you need a subject refresher or if you are intimidated by the subject material.
3. Join a research group that will net you credits in chemistry, math, biology or physics as they will contribute to your science GPA.

CHAPTER FOURTEEN

Student Council

If you want to squeeze every drop of value out of your BYU experience while also learning team building, patience, and leadership, joining student council is a great option for you. At BYU, you have the option of being involved in student council on both the university level and at the college level. The ten colleges that make up BYU are:

- Business
- Education
- Engineering and Technology
- Family, Home and Social Sciences
- Fine Arts and Communications
- Graduate Studies
- Humanities
- Life Sciences
- Nursing
- Physical and Mathematical Sciences

College-Level Student Councils

While each college's student council has its own unique mission statement and objectives, they all focus on helping to enrich the educational, service, and networking opportunities available to the students of their college. Ben served on the College of Humanities Student Council for four semesters, and during that time, the council worked very hard to help advertise humanities minors to non-humanities students as well as help humanities majors get involved with non-humanities disciplines in an effort to become more rounded scholars. To achieve their purpose, Ben and the rest of the council organized events, produced and distributed advertisements, and even put on clinics to help students prepare their elevator pitches and resumes for the BYU career fair.

University-Level Student Council (BYUSA)

The BYU Student Association (BYUSA) was established almost 30 years ago with the purpose of "serving others so that there are no intellectually, spiritually, emotionally, or physically poor among us"[164] and accomplishes this through managing dozens of student clubs, school dances, and other various volunteer and social events throughout the year.

BYUSA is analogous to other universities' student body governments but with a couple of key differences. At many universities, the student governing body has the power to create school bylaws, policies, and procedures. The governing student body usually has the ability to apply pressure on the school administration in behalf of the student body. This ensures that the student body always has a powerful voice and is taken into consideration when important decisions are being made at the administrative level.

BYUSA functions in a similar role discerning and voicing the opinions and concerns of the student body to the administration. However, BYUSA serves more as a

---

[164] "Home." *Student Leadership*. Web. 28 February 2018. <https://BYUsa.BYU.edu/>.

sounding board than a governing body with legislative power. Therefore, it does not have the same amount of leverage with the administration as the more traditional student governments do.

For a real-life example of the differences between traditional university student governments and BYUSA let's look at BYU Dining Services' policy to not sell caffeinated beverages on BYU campus for decades up until late 2017. While students were free to bring their own caffeine, there was no place on campus where students could purchase caffeinated drinks. The 'caffeine desert' extended to the various off-campus BYU Creameries scattered around Provo as well as the BYU LaVell Edwards football stadium and Marriott Center basketball arena.

At other universities, if the majority of the student body was in support, the student government could have pressured the administration to make caffeine available for purchase on campus. Not so at BYU. While Ben was serving on the BYUSA Student Advisory Council, it was made very clear on the first day of class that attempts to make any changes to the caffeine policy or Honor Code would not be entertained.

While BYU's caffeine policy reversal came as a complete surprise to us, the possibility that the student body had any sway in the matter is extremely unlikely as Ben's experience as a member of the Student Advisory Council illustrates.

Despite these differences, BYUSA offers a tremendous number of wonderful opportunities for students to serve and help affect positive change on campus.

For practical purposes, BYUSA can be broken into two separate parts with different roles that are united with the same purpose. One of these halves consists of various service programs and organizations. The other is BYU's version of a student council.

On the volunteer side, students participate in one or more of the many volunteer organizations sponsored by BYUSA. Students involved in these volunteer activities gain leadership experience, build camaraderie with fellow volunteers, and provide amazing service to the community and the needy (see chapter 12: Service Opportunities).

On the leadership side, each year a few students will be selected for one of the top student leadership positions within BYUSA. These student officers include a President and an Executive Vice President, who are both voted into office by the student body during yearly elections in the same fashion our national presidential elections work. Seven other vice presidents each oversee specific organizations including clubs, Y-Activities, etc. Twenty-one students serve as executive directors under the direction of the seven vice presidents and assist them with running the organizations they oversee.

In addition to the Student President and Executive Vice President is a separate council of students known as the Student Advisory Council (SAC). Whereas the majority of other BYUSA officers are focused on the everyday operations of specific organizations within BYUSA, SAC is composed of students representing each college, and it serves as the voice of the entire student body to the faculty and administration. SAC meets and works very closely with many top BYU administrators, including the office of the University President and various university Vice Presidents. SAC members are often used as a sounding board from which the administration can get student feedback about various proposals or important issues before they are finalized or brought before the general student body.

Participation in BYUSA can be an incredibly fulfilling way to expand and enrich your undergraduate experience at BYU. Whether you choose to serve in one of the many volunteer programs or decide to apply for one of the leadership positions, BYUSA has a spot for you! If you are interested in a role in student leadership, be sure to get involved as early as possible. Some of the positions, like Student President and Executive Vice President, require a significant BYUSA leadership experience before you can be eligible. Check out the BYUSA office and webpage for more information about the various programs and organizations available to you.

Call to Action

1. Get information about your college's student council from your academic advisement center.
2. If you are interested in BYUSA, get involved as early as possible as several positions like BYUSA President and Vice President require you have prior experience working within the BYUSA program.

CHAPTER FIFTEEN

On-Campus Resources

At BYU, you have access to an incredible array of different on-campus resources ranging from assistance with your upcoming paper at the Writing Center to help with filing your taxes, and almost every offered service and resource is available to you for free! Most BYU students are completely unaware of many of these excellent resources. We want to introduce you to some of the commonly underutilized resources and have listed them below. Regularly review this list so that you don't miss out.

Academic Success Center

The Academic Success Center (ASC)[165] offers a host of great programs, assessments, and workshops. These programs are designed to develop skills that will help you excel at both your student and future endeavors. Daily workshop topics include communication, listening and note taking, memory, stress management, test preparation, textbook comprehension, and time management.[166] The ASC also

---

[165] "Learning Mentoring." *Academic Success Center*. Web. 28 February 2018. <https://casc.BYU.edu/>.

[166] "Academic Success Center." *ASC Workshops*. Web. 28 February 2018. <https://casc.byu.edu/workshops>.

offers a variety of personality and interest assessments. Most of these assessments are free, but a few do incur a modest fee. Several of these tests are specially designed to help match you with majors and careers that would likely be interesting to you and are a great way to discover possible career options that you may have never considered before.

The ASC also features quite a few student development courses. These courses are taken for credit just like a normal class but are designed like workshops and will help you build the skill set you need to accomplish your goals as an undergraduate student. The ASC website describes the purpose of these courses with the following list.

Student Development courses are designed to help you:

- Raise your grade point average
- Be an effective decision maker
- Improve performance on exams with better test-taking skills
- Make reading a meaningful experience
- Handle note-taking challenges
- Create strategies to deal with the expectations found in college
- Explore and identify a major that is suited to your interests, values, and plans
- Face the university experience with greater confidence
- Recognize your developing personality and strengths
- Grow in personal development as a college student

For a full list of student development classes being offered, see the ASC website.[167] The ASC webpage also has links to many other valuable resources, including a link to scholarship databases, internship and career networks, major searches, and even financial planning.

Counseling and Psychological Services

Counseling and Psychological Services[168] exists to provide students with important services including screening, individual counseling, group therapy, marital therapy, online self-help, substance abuse prevention and treatment, and more. You can make an appointment by phone or on the Counseling and Psychological Services webpage.

Financial Fitness Center

Be sure to take the time to peruse the Financial Fitness Center webpage[169] where you will find helpful information about making a personalized financial plan, smart spending, managing student loans, and establishing credit along with dozens of other helpful articles, videos, and financial tools. There is even a detailed guide to buying textbooks on a budget!

Subject Librarians

A little-known fact is that students can set up an appointment and get one-on-one help from subject librarians

---

[167] "University Advisement Center." *Student Development Classes*. Web. 28 February 2018. <https://universityadvisement.byu.edu/student-development-classes>.

[168] "Counseling and Psychological Services." *Counseling and Psychological Services*. Web. 28 February 2018. <https://caps.BYU.edu/>.

[169] "Student Center for Financial Management & Planning." *Student Center for Financial Management & Planning*. Web. 28 February 2018. <https://financialplan.BYU.edu/>.

at the HBLL.[170] These special librarians are experts and know absolutely everything there is to know about the library books and resources relating to their specific subject. Subject librarians are an invaluable resource when doing research on a specific topic or genre or just looking for a particular book located somewhere in their part of the library. There are over a hundred unique subject librarians ready to help students get the most out of the HBLL. A list of subject librarians can be found on the HBLL webpage.[171]

Tutorial Labs

Many departments on campus have one or more tutorial labs where you can go to get one-on-one help with your homework or get questions answered outside of your normal class hours. These labs are staffed by highly qualified undergraduate and graduate students who have taken and achieved high marks in the very classes you are seeking

---

[170] The Harold B. Lee Library (HBLL) is nationally recognized for its size—i.e., number of holdings and miles, yes miles, of shelf space—and is regularly listed as being among the best college libraries in the United States. See, for instance, "The 20 Best College Libraries in 2017." *Best Colleges*. 07 Apr. 2017. Web. 28 February 2018. <http://www.bestcolleges.com/features/the-best-college-libraries/>, and "The 50 Most Amazing College Libraries." *College Rank*. Web. 28 February 2018. <http://www.collegerank.net/amazing-college-libraries/>, and "The Top 50 Largest College Libraries in the U.S." *CollegeXpress*.Web. 28 February 2018. <http://www.collegexpress.com/lists/list/the-top-50-largest-college-libraries-in-the-us/747/>. The Harold, as the library is affectionately called, even enjoyed the fame generated by a spoof of an Old Spice commercial that went viral back in 2010. It's definitely worth watching again and again, if only to get a glimpse of that celestial sandwich. As of 28 February 2018, the video entitled *New Spice | Study Like a Scholar, Scholar* had been viewed a total of 3,519,139 times. If you tried to watch it that many times in a row, it would take you just over 1,943 days! "New Spice | Study like a Scholar, Scholar." *YouTube*. 15 July 2010. Web. 28 February 2018. <https://youtu.be/2ArIj236UHs>.

[171] "Research Guides." *BYU Library*. Web. 28 February 2018. <https://lib.BYU.edu/guides/#subjectguides>.

help with. The tutorial labs are also a great place to find and study with other students working on the same assignments or preparing for the same exams as you. Countless students have found these help labs invaluable as they work to master difficult material. Below is a list of departments with one or more help labs:

- Biology
- Chemistry and Biochemistry
- Math
- Multimedia (for help with graphic design, web design, and audio and video production) [172]
- Physics and Astronomy
- Physical Science

Pre Professional Advisement Center

Are you interested in a career in medicine, dentistry, law, or business? If so, the Pre Professional Advisement Center (PPAC)[173] can be an excellent resource as you are mapping out your undergraduate classes, deciding which extracurriculars to take part in, and preparing to take the appropriate standardized tests. At the PPAC, you can get detailed information about the process of gaining admittance into the postgraduate school of your dreams as well as receive help planning out the necessary steps to get you there. On top of all that, you can get valuable information about shadowing professionals in your field of interest, volunteer opportunities, job opportunities, and even help with applications.

---

[172] "HBLL Multimedia Lab." *Multimedia Lab Information.* Web. 28 February 2018. <https://mmlab.lib.BYU.edu/mmlab/info.php>.

[173] "Pre Professional Advisement Center." *Student Development Classes for Prehealth Students.* Web. 28 February 2018. <https://ppa.BYU.edu/classes>.

The advisement center also offers student development classes, which are a great way for you to preview your future career as you meet and interact with actual professionals in a class setting each week. These fantastic introductory courses are available to all students, and each class has a specific emphasis on one topic such as health professions, physician assistant, dentistry, medicine, optometry, and others. There are also classes with an emphasis on helping students learn advanced reading strategies, participate in relevant internships, and complete their medical or dental school application. Taking a few of these classes along with talking to an advisor are great ways to see if a career in medicine, law, or business is right for you.

Research and Writing Center

At the Research and Writing Center[174] you can schedule a time to meet one-on-one with research consultants and writing tutors. These consultants and tutors will help you learn how to use the HBLL resources to do research and improve your writing. A trip to the Research and Writing Center can help you level up a B paper into an A paper. The Research and Writing Center webpage explains what help you can receive.

Research consultants can help with:

- Selecting and narrowing a topic
- Finding research sources
- Storing and citing your sources
- Referring you to subject experts to help with additional or specialized research needs

---

[174] "Frequently Asked Questions." *Frequently Asked Questions: Is There a Research and Writing Center in the Library? What Are the Hours?* Web. 28 February 2018. <http://ask.lib.BYU.edu/a.php?qid=109003>.

Writing Tutors can help with:

- Ensuring that the writing matches the assignment
- Clarifying, solidifying, and strengthening content
- Organizing the text
- Identifying and working with grammar and usage concerns
- Citing sources and following a specific format (e.g., APA)
- Dealing with writer's block
- Discussing document design
- Revising for stylistic considerations

Women's Services and Resources

The on-campus Women's Services and Resources center (WSR)[175] has a wide variety of resources and programs available for dealing with difficulties as well as for education and empowerment. These resources are available to all members of the BYU community, including men who are interested in women's topics. The WSR is equipped to help students address issues ranging from eating disorders to family and career balance to individuality and divine worth.[176]

The WSR webpage has links to many of the different resources and programs available through the WSR, including a list of women's clubs and scholarships for single-parent or nontraditional students. The WSR also offers nutrition and wellness consultations by appointment and almost a dozen different workshops focused on empowering women, relationships, and wellness and nutrition.

---

[175] "Women's Services & Resources." *Women's Services & Resources*. Web. 28 February 2018. <https://wsr.BYU.edu/>.

[176] "Women's Services & Resources." *What Is WSR?* Web. 28 February 2018. <https://wsr.BYU.edu/content/what-wsr>.

Additionally, the WSR hosts free yoga classes and other regular events. Check out the WSR webpage for volunteer opportunities, links to the WSR blog, and information about how men can get involved with the WSR.

Multicultural Student Services

The Multicultural Student Services (MSS)[177] office aims to develop an environment of "fellow citizenry where multiculturalism can flourish."[178] The MSS office accomplishes this goal by providing a full portfolio of programs and services. This is emphasized by the MSS mission to serve minority students and the university community at BYU as a whole. The MSS will:

- Advise in academic, cultural, financial, social, and personal needs
- Foster leadership development and opportunities
- Provide cultural events which educate and include all students
- Track academic progress of students
- Sponsor college preparation programs

The MSS office also provides programs to help prospective BYU students prepare for and excel at BYU by participating in the Summer of Academic Refinement (SOAR) program. Through the SOAR program, participants are given mentorship, exposure to BYU campus and facilities, and ACT test preparation.

---

[177] "Home." *Multicultural Student Services*. Web. 28 February 2018. <https://multicultural.byu.edu/>.

[178] "Mission." *Multicultural Student Services*. Web. 28 February 2018. <https://multicultural.BYU.edu/content/mission>.

Some of the most exciting programs offered by the MSS are the different cultural events that highlight some of the exciting and exotic cultures of BYU students. These events allow participants to learn about and celebrate different cultures. Cultural events that have been hosted in the past include a fiesta focused on Central and Latin American cultures, Black History Month celebrations, pow wows, and luaus.

International Student Services

The International Student Services (ISS)[179] office is an invaluable resource for international students at BYU. The ISS helps international students understand and navigate sometimes tricky issues like type of legal status, employment eligibility, passports, and academic requirements. The ISS also has information regarding scholarships, tax information, admissions, visas, and more. If you are an international student, be sure to work closely with the ISS to ensure a smooth and successful experience at BYU.

University Accessibility Center

The University Accessibility Center (UAC)[180] offers services for BYU students with disabilities. The aim of the UAC is to ensure that students with disabilities are able to excel at BYU in every way possible. The UAC has services and programs available for students who are deaf and hard of hearing or who have emotional disabilities, learning disabilities, ADD/ADHD disorder, physical disabilities, chronic illness, or visual disabilities. The UAC website even

---

[179] "International Student and Scholar Services." *International Student and Scholar Services*. Web. 28 February 2018. <https://internationalservices.BYU.edu/>.

[180] "Home." *University Accessibility Center*. Web. 28 February 2018. <https://uac.BYU.edu/>.

has a link to scholarships dedicated to students with disabilities.

Y-Be-Fit

Y-Be-Fit (YBF)[181] is a wellness clinic that offers its services to BYU staff, faculty, administration, and students. The staff members there are friendly and knowledgeable and can help you achieve your health and fitness goals. The clinic offers a three-month program or services a la carte, such as body composition testing in the bod pod, a spiffy and futuristic looking capsule that estimates the proportion of fat mass to lean mass using—warning! big words ahead—*air displacement plethysmography*. (Try saying that ten times in a row without messing up!) In addition, you can get inexpensive nutritional analyses, blood lipid profiles, and blood glucose tests through YBF.

YBF staff members are not usually certified personal trainers, and one-on-one personal training goes beyond the scope of the program, but a skilled and knowledgeable YBF staff member should be able to put together a basic cardio program or strength training program to help you stay in shape as you pursue your studies.

If you are studying in the exercise science, health sciences, or nutrition and dietetics departments, take a look at working at YBF during your undergraduate to fulfill internship hours or to get a feel for health and wellness coaching as a possible career path.

Call to Action

1. Regularly skim through this chapter to make sure you don't forget about the many on-campus resources that are available to you.

---

[181] "Home." *Y Be Fit*. Web. 28 February 2018. <https://ybefit.BYU.edu/>.

2. Pick an on-campus resource that you think would be useful but you haven't utilized yet. Go down to the office or make an appointment for a visit and see what the resource can do for you.

Conclusion

We hope you found this book helpful and that it has proved to be a useful guide for you. We know that everyone will have a unique experience as a student at BYU, but if our book helped you learn about and get involved in even just one new program or activity, we will feel like we accomplished our mission in writing it.

Our purpose is to help future and current BYU students increase their productivity during their undergraduate years. We've included a lot of tips, but we want to again emphasize the importance of having mentors. Mentors help us see opportunities that we might not at present see, helping us to chart our course with increased success.

There was no way we could include everything that BYU has to offer in this book, which is why we invite you to share with us anything we missed. Visit www.acingbyu.com and https://www.facebook.com/acingBYU/ and share with us your experiences and the lessons you've learned that you think other students will benefit from. Then invite your family and friends—past, present, and future BYU students—to share too. Together, we will give the gift of mentorship.

Once you are finished with your undergraduate years and have joined the distinguished ranks of BYU alumni, we encourage you to take the time to find a way to mentor and help younger students as they work hard, encountering both successes and failures. Sometimes, just an encouraging word can be enough for frustrated students to recommit themselves to attending class and being more diligent about studying for tests. Like the proverbial butterfly whose wings beat here only to cause a typhoon across the globe, as a mentor you never know how much influence your words and actions have on others.

Go forth and serve!

About the Authors

Ben Black

After returning from the Japan Tokyo Mission in 2010, Ben got his start at BYU first as a visiting student and then as a transfer student. With Nate's help, Ben secured a spot as an undergraduate researcher working in an Exercise Science lab. He found the experience so rewarding that he went on to do research in analytical chemistry, library and information studies, ecology, and Japanese, and he co-authored several publications. For both an ORCA Grant and his Honors Thesis, Ben examined the link between foreign language study and the formation of long-term memory. Aside from research, Ben served on the College of Humanities Student Council for two years and on the BYUSA Student Advisory Council for one year. During his senior year, he interned with Emmersion Learning. Outside of school, Ben worked at the Missionary Training Center teaching Japanese before starting a personal training business. Since graduating with BYU Honors in 2016 with a Bachelor of Arts degree in Japanese and a minor in chemistry, Ben has been pursuing a career in the military and in medicine.

Nate Black

After two years of service in the Samoa Apia Mission, Nate returned to BYU and was awarded a Bachelor of Science degree in Exercise Sciences: Fitness and Wellness Management in 2006 and a Master of Science degree in Exercise Sciences: Exercise Physiology in 2009. During his undergraduate studies, Nate was a Resident Assistant in Helaman Halls for two years. He was also an intern at Y-Be-Fit for two years and one of its graduate student co-directors for another one and a half years. After BYU, Nate attended the University of Hawaii at Manoa where he earned a Master of Science degree in Nutritional Sciences in 2012. Between 2011 and 2014, he taught second-year Samoan language and introductory nutrition courses at the University of Hawaii at Manoa. Nate still doesn't know what he wants to be when he grows up. He wishes he could go back in time and mentor himself through his under-graduate years. In the meantime, Nate enjoys reading and listening to as many books as he can find time for.

Index

CPSIA information can be obtained
at www.ICGtesting.com
Printed in the USA
FFOW03n2340300518
46969979-49256FF

9 780692 057131